Canadian Literature in English

VOLUME ONE

W. J. Keith

Canadian Literature in English

REVISED AND EXPANDED EDITION

Volume One

The Porcupine's Quill

Library and Archives Canada Cataloguing in Publication

Keith, W. J. (William John), 1934–
Canadian literature in English / W. J. Keith. – Rev. ed.

Includes bibliographies and index.
ISBN-13: 978-0-88984-283-0 (v. 1)
ISBN-13: 978-0-88984-285-4 (v. 2)

1. Canadian literature (English) – History and criticism.
I. Title.

PS8071.K45 2006   C810'.9   C2006-904471-6

Published by The Porcupine's Quill, 68 Main St, Erin, Ontario NOB 1TO.
http://www.sentex.net/~pql

Readied for the press by John Metcalf.
Copy edited by Doris Cowan.

Represented in Canada by the Literary Press Group.
Trade orders are available from University of Toronto Press.

We acknowledge the support of the Ontario Arts Council and the Canada
Council for the Arts for our publishing program. The financial support of the
Government of Canada through the Book Publishing Industry Development
Program is also gratefully acknowledged. Thanks, also, to the Government
of Ontario through the Ontario Media Development Corporation's
OMDC Book Fund.

 Canada Council
for the Arts

Conseil des Arts
du Canada

ONTARIO ARTS COUNCIL
CONSEIL DES ARTS DE L'ONTARIO

Canada is a very peculiar and different country.
— James Reaney

TRUEMAN: A weight of tradition may be as great a handicap as none at all.
LOVEWIT: But a genuine, living tradition is constantly renewing itself.
— Robertson Davies

Our writing cannot help but be Canadian, don't let us ever worry about that. But it can be good or bad. That is what matters.
— Ethel Wilson

We're all part of a tradition, and if we don't show responsibility to the tradition ... the whole damn thing's going to collapse.
— John Metcalf

Table of Contents

References

To avoid excessive footnoting, references have been incorporated into the text. Details for shortened entries will be found readily enough in 'Further Reading' at the end of Volume Two, under the individual author discussed, the author of the quotation (if a notable Canadian writer), or the appropriate subsections ('Interviews', 'Fiction', etc.).

Abbreviations

ABCMA: *Annotated Bibliography of Canada's Major Authors*. For details, see 'Further Reading: Reference Books'.

CEECT: Centre for Editing Early Canadian Texts (Ottawa: Carleton University Press).

CCP: Canadian Poetry Press (London, Ontario).

CWTW: *Canadian Writers and Their Works*. For details, see 'Further Reading: Reference Books'.

DLB: *Dictionary of Literary Biography*. For details, see 'Further Reading: Reference Books'.

ECW: Either *Essays on Canadian Writing*, an academic journal, or ECW Press, a publishing company which grew out of the journal.

LHC: *Literary History of Canada*. For details, see 'Further Reading: Reference Books'.

M&S: McClelland and Stewart, 'the Canadian Publishers' (Toronto).

MQUP: McGill-Queens University Press (Montréal).

NCL: New Canadian Library (M&S).

OUP: Oxford University Press (Toronto branch).

PCL: *Profiles in Canadian Literature*. For details, see 'Further Reading: Reference Books'.

UTP: University of Toronto Press.

UTQ: *University of Toronto Quarterly*.

Preface (1985)

This book contains one man's reading of Canadian literature in English from its earliest beginnings. It lays its emphasis firmly on cultural tradition, the way in which literature written in Canada began as a continuation of what was being produced in Great Britain, had to define itself against the American tradition as it developed in the United States, and eventually evolved as a distinctive literature related to but independent of both parent and neighbour. Obviously, Canada's geography and her historical development were immensely influential factors, and these will be discussed briefly in the introductory chapter. But the concept of a 'Canadian tradition' is not easily established. In literary terms it is, I believe, neither an abstraction like a sense of identity nor a theme like survival. It evolves gradually from the achieved works of literary art that have been written by its people. I have tried to approach my task without narrowing preoccupations, describing what I found by focusing on writing that attains a high level of literary quality. While attempting to survey works of continuing interest, this book concentrates unabashedly on the mainstream; it emphasizes authors who may be considered 'major' because they have dominated the country's literary language, shaped its consciousness, and so fostered the native tradition. Ultimately, I am convinced, it is the tradition established by the best that sets the standard.

Inevitably I have had to be highly selective. There are far more writers of merit than could be included unless parts of the book were to degenerate into little more than a list of names. This is particularly true of the contemporary period, although non-Canadian readers may still be surprised by the amount of attention paid to literature produced after 1950. But the pattern of Canadian literary development consists of a long slow growth followed by a sudden creative burgeoning. Indeed, it seems reasonable to suppose that the majority of Canadian writers up to the present whose work will prove of continuing interest in the future are alive now.* Many of these, naturally, are at an early stage in their careers,

---

* This is no longer true; see 'Preface to the Revised Edition'.

and because of my special concern with cultural continuity I have concentrated on the present-day writers whose debt to the past is most obvious. Some notable experimentalists have doubtless been scanted in the process, but the concept of tradition is constantly revisionist, and, if they prove to be of lasting importance and succeed in altering or refining the tradition, they will eventually come into their own. I shall be satisfied if I have distinguished, albeit superficially, some of the main lines of an intricate literary development.

One practical problem always confronts the writer on early Canada: what does 'Canada' mean at any given point in time? The country's present boundaries were not established until after the Second World War. At various times new administrative units have been created; names (Upper Canada, Canada West, Ontario, for example) can change with changing circumstances or the whims of politicians. While I have sometimes reminded readers of these anomalies in phrases like 'what is now Saskatchewan', I have thought it best to refer for convenience to Canada as we know it today. E. J. Pratt was surely Canadian despite the fact that Newfoundland was a separate colony when he was born there. The risk of occasionally blurring through imprecision is, in my view, outweighed by the general advantage of simplicity and straightforwardness. So long as the reader is alerted to the difficulty at the outset, few problems should result.

Very occasionally, when referring to authors and books that I have previously discussed in print, I found that I could not improve upon certain phrases and sentences that I have published in articles and reviews. With these small exceptions, all the material in this book appears for the first time.

An unavoidable difficulty in describing and assessing a literature most impressive in its contemporary achievements is that works are continually being published that deserve attention and alter the general picture. I have tried to keep as up to date as possible, but readers should know that the body of the text was written between June 1982 and June 1983.

As usual there are debts I am happy to acknowledge. First and foremost, I am grateful to the Connaught Committee of the University of Toronto for the award of a Connaught Senior Fellowship that gave me a year's release from teaching duties, during which I wrote the bulk of the book. The General Editors of the Longman Literature in English series, under whose auspices the book first appeared, were most helpful and patient in offering advice, while colleagues too numerous to mention individually have been prodigal with interest and encouragement. And, as always, I am grateful to my wife, Hiroko, not only because she is an excellent proofreader but also because for many years we have explored Canadian literature together.

– *W. J. Keith*, 1985

Preface to the Revised Edition

When I was invited to revise and update this book in 2004, nineteen years after its original publication, my first thought was that it would have to be totally rewritten. Further consideration, however, revealed that it was completed, in Sam Solecki's words in *The Last Canadian Poet* when writing of Al Purdy's poetic career, at 'the close of the major phase of the Canadian literary tradition' (xiv). Since then the basic pattern has changed little. Indeed, the only obviously outdated statement in the above preface is the claim that 'the majority of Canadian writers up to the present time whose work will prove of continuing interest in the future are alive now'. Of the individual authors listed in the original bibliography, more than thirty have died since 1985. Moreover, for various reasons, several of which will be discussed in the concluding chapter of the second volume, although a considerable number of younger writers have appeared on the scene, few have displayed unequivocal claims to major status. The remarkable flowering that began to manifest itself in the middle of the twentieth century had run its course by the beginning of the new millennium.

As a result, the general shape of the book requires little alteration. A number of writers who had already achieved stature maintained their reputations, but only a few extended them. I have therefore decided to confine myself to minimal changes in the main body of the text. These include the correction of a few errors, a number of stylistic refinements, and some alterations and additions rendered necessary by the passing of time. I have left the main arguments and evaluations as they were. For technical reasons, however, the order of Parts 3 and 4 has been reversed for this edition.

The *apparatus criticus* (also in the second volume) has, however, been completely revised and revamped to meet current needs – though not to reflect current fashion. I have deliberately avoided jargon, 'theory', and the criticism embracing them for reasons given in detail in an added Appendix. A year-by-year 'chronology' has been dropped in favour of more extended recommendations for further reading that not only include listings of recent work but also record the presence of biographies and scholarly editions which did not exist in the early 1980s.

Once again, I must repeat that the book was highly selective in 1985, and stress that the coverage of twenty years of further writing means that it is now more selective than ever. Much worthy and effective writing has had to be passed over in silence. In the main, I have ignored the 'popular' at one extreme (no mention of Lucy Maud Montgomery or Robert Service) and left the 'avant-garde' to look after itself at the other (no mention of bp Nichol or Anne Carson). If this is a damaging admission on my part, so be it; the more adventurous are free to venture further.

Finally, I have endeavoured to lay stress on those writings that I consider a pleasure to read, especially though not exclusively for the pleasure of their style. Despite the trendy popularity of the phrase 'the pleasures of the text' a few years ago, 'pleasure' is a word that does not occur regularly in contemporary literary discussion. For my part, I read literature unashamedly for pleasure – not the 'fun' so distressingly flaunted by bureaucratic committees of adult education, but *pleasure*. So far as Canadian literature is concerned, this book is a report on what has pleased me. I dedicate it to all those (including the general reading public whose endangered status is lamented in the 'Polemical Conclusion') who recognize and respond to the dance of words.

– *W. J. Keith*, 2005

Introduction

Canada. A country stretching over 3,000 miles (some 5,500 kilometres) from east to west and sometimes extending almost 3,000 miles from south to north, though most of its northern lands are unsettled and uninhabitable. In area the second largest country in the world, with a population more or less half that of the United Kingdom. A country with two official languages, English and French, and many unofficial. A country that shares its vast east-west boundary with an English-speaking, culturally aggressive nation-state boasting approximately ten times its population. A country in which the native peoples (Indian and Inuit) now constitute less than 2 per cent of its total inhabitants. A country of close to 4 million square miles in which over three-quarters of the population live in towns and cities. A country which began to come together as a stable political unit in 1867 and whose present boundaries were established as recently as 1949. A country whose written history spans no more than five hundred years (John Cabot entered the Gulf of St. Lawrence in 1497), and whose English literary tradition can hardly be traced back further than the middle of the eighteenth century.

So extensive and rugged a country could be settled only gradually. At first, white communities consisted of isolated trading posts and military garrisons, with scattered settlements (French and English) in the eastern parts of the land. In the seventeenth century, most of the activity was French, with the English-speaking colonies more prominent in the areas to the south. A little later, increasing imperial ambitions led to an inevitable clash between the two main powers interested in the control of North America. The defeat of the French by the English, ensured by Wolfe's victory over Montcalm on the Plains of Abraham in 1759, resulted in a brief period, effectively little more than a decade, when most of settled North America was British. However, the American revolution soon followed, and it left Canada in a curiously anomalous position. At that time it consisted of a series of (more or less) loyal communities which preferred to align themselves with Britain than with the infant United States but which, from the beginning, sought to establish a viable society that modified British social and political customs without hurrying into the extreme experiment of immediate independence.

The establishment of the United States as a separate country led to a notable influx of 'Loyalists' into the Canadian maritime colonies, and it was this nucleus of immigrants and settlers, unwilling to sever connections with the mother country, that laid the foundation – at once social, political, and psychological – for what eventually cohered as the Canadian nation. But the province of Québec, where Loyalists had also settled, was at the same time in a state of crucial transition. As early as 1791 the Canada Act had divided this area into Upper and Lower Canada (the former primarily English-speaking) and the War of 1812, in which inhabitants of both Canadas successfully resisted expansionist tendencies from south of the border, did much to foster a sense of corporate distinctiveness. In particular, the uneasy period of forced readjustment in Europe after the close of the Napoleonic Wars saw increased British immigration to Canada on a massive scale. The society of Ontario (at first Upper Canada, then Canada West) began to take shape during this period. Further west, however, the land was still wild, only sporadically and sparsely settled, and for the most part not even mapped, though the efforts of the Hudson's Bay and North West Companies had given the area considerable commercial importance.

But Canada was not and could never be a mere copy of Britain reproduced on the other side of the Atlantic. Changes of all kinds were inevitable. The unsuccessful but disturbing rebellions in Upper and Lower Canada in 1837 gave evidence of substantial political unrest, and resulted in Lord Durham's famous Report (1839), which eased the way towards responsible government. This and the increased awareness of the possibilities of western expansion clearly demonstrated the need for unification of British North America, and a series of conferences duly led in 1867 to 'Confederation', the creation of the Dominion of Canada originally made up of New Brunswick, Nova Scotia, Ontario, and Québec. These provinces were soon joined in 1870 by Manitoba (created after the controversial handing over of power from the Hudson's Bay Company and the defeat of the first Riel Rebellion), in 1871 by British Columbia (whose entry depended on the promised completion of a transcontinental railway), and in 1873 by Prince Edward Island. The western prairies, previously administered as part of the Northwest Territories, were reorganized into the provinces of Alberta and Saskatchewan in 1905. Finally, as I have already noted, Newfoundland joined Confederation to complete the nation's current boundaries in 1949. With political responsibilities divided between the central federal government and the ten provincial governments, plus the Yukon, the Northwest Territories, and the recently proclaimed – primarily Inuit – Nunavut (1999), Canada remains to this day a curious amalgam by which a combination of flexibility and reluctant compromise has over the years proved to be a source of frustrating weakness but also of paradoxical and even endearing strength.

This ambiguous compromise is also conspicuous in the history of Canadian literature. Until fairly recently, the vast majority of the population was either British or French in ethnic origin, though other peoples now constitute well over a quarter of the total. Naturally, this majority looked back to Britain and France for its intellectual and literary sustenance. And just as naturally, in the case of English-speaking Canada, the influence of the energetic and populous United States (in recent years most conspicuous through radio, film, and television – not to mention the Internet – but from early times to the present no less significantly through newspapers and books) was considerable. The Americans, of course, had a far greater stimulus to produce an alternative and distinctive literature in English. Since they had become an independent nation, it was a logical step to define the difference between Britain and the United States in literary as well as other terms. But because Canada had not severed political ties, there was less reason to break literary connections; the incentive to produce an independent national literature that might stand as both a foundation and a symbol was thus comparatively weak. Besides, the majority of the early immigrants were practical-minded settlers with little time or inclination for artistic and intellectual pursuits; the Moodies and the Traills were very much exceptions to the general rule. The conservative character of the Canadian experiment is also manifest here. Pioneering was considered praiseworthy in matters of everyday living, but not in the arts; it was in the virgin forests, not in literature, that trails were to be blazed.

There were other even more practical barriers. Not only was a leisured class barely existent, but the scattered communities spread across immense distances dissipated whatever impetus to literary and cultural pursuits might have developed. The economics of printing and distributing local books in such a situation were virtually prohibitive; books were only needed in small numbers, cartage rates were high, even bookshops few and far between. British and American publishers, on the other hand, were able to produce their own popular items in such quantities that the price could be kept low, and whatever Canadian market existed could be adequately· served. Copyright arrangements (or the lack of them) also worked against the interests of potential Canadian writers. These were daunting obstacles, and some of them still remain in place. Only those Canadians who reach international best-seller lists can be distributed in Canada on equal financial terms with successful foreign authors. This is a plight shared by many countries with small populations, but it has been exacerbated in Canada's case by the fact that her rivals within the same language have produced some of the finest literature in the modern world.

In such circumstances, it may seem almost quixotic to speak of a Canadian literary tradition; indeed, a number of critics and commentators have offered seductive reasons – some mutually contradictory – why the concept is untenable. The psychological effects of a colonial past, a narrow and emotionally crippling puritanism, excessive openness to foreign influences (or, sometimes, an obstinate and parochial rejection of them), the supposed dullness of Canada and the Canadian people, a 'lack of ghosts' (Earle Birney's phrase in 'Can. Lit.'), the lack of an authentic history: all these have been isolated, dissected, brooded upon. And ironically a tradition of criticism assuming (sometimes with regret, sometimes almost with satisfaction) the absence of tradition has grown up and established itself. This critical assumption is, I am convinced, unjustified – and an explanation becomes evident in any firm scrutiny of the last item on my list, the claimed lack of an authentic history. Such a claim is obviously false: it referred, in fact, to the recent appearance of *white* peoples upon the scene and their reliance upon *written* history. The literary form of the argument could be argued cogently (though not, in the last analysis, convincingly) up to some fifty years ago but has long since become outdated.

The remarkable activity in Canada since the Second World War has, of course, been recognized and celebrated by literary criticism (which has itself multiplied in conspicuous, even alarming fashion), but the critical presuppositions derived from an earlier period have remained curiously entrenched. Partly as a cause, partly as an effect of this situation, the critical emphasis until comparatively recently has been upon thematic studies assessing the artistic treatment of what are considered notably Canadian preoccupations, or on detailed discussions of individual writers. Canadian literature has surprisingly seldom been viewed in terms of any consistent historical continuity. Nor are there many generic studies to demonstrate the debt, in poetry or fiction or whatever, of one literary generation to another. The existence of a Canadian tradition has sometimes been asserted, sometimes questioned, but rarely explored with any care.

This critical hiatus has occurred, I believe, because individual investigators have experienced a clash of loyalties and priorities. Alongside the natural desire to foster and encourage a growing literature went a corresponding fear that this new creative burgeoning might be stifled by the burden of a traditional past, especially if the traditions in question came from outside the country. Aware of, and embarrassed by, the general conservatism of nineteenth-century Canadian literature, its technical and formal timidity, its derivativeness from primarily British models (though not, as we shall see, without gradually evolving independent features), they found the whole concept of tradition questionable. Besides, the nation was struggling to assert its own independent identity – the word is a Canadian favourite – at a time of increasing economic dependence on the United States. In Canada's literary productions, emphasis fell on the contemporary achievement; its ancestry, its lines of development, its relations to the larger context of literature in English, went for the most part unexamined.

I would argue, however, that the Canadian literary tradition is now sufficiently established that it can be discussed in relation to the literature of Britain and the United States without embarrassment and without any nagging sense of cultural inferiority. Thus the British tradition can now be recognized not as an imperialistic burden to be discarded but as an example – not one to be meekly imitated, of course, but to be cherished and even enhanced. However independent Canada may now have become, the British connection remains an essential element in our past with palpable effects upon our present – not least, of course, in the use of the English language. Similarly, while there are currently reasons to view it with some defensive unease, the American literary achievement is better seen not negatively as a threatening force but as a parallel yet different and stimulating offshoot. Indeed, this metaphor of branches growing out from an original tree (or of children gradually becoming independent of a parent) has constantly been employed in discussions of Canadian literature in English since the latter part of the nineteenth century. Recently it seems to have fallen into disfavour – another manifestation, no doubt, of a newly asserted independence; none the less, in my view it remains apt.

As the above discussion implies, the years between the mid-1960s and the mid-1980s saw the emergence of a distinctively patriotic movement within Canadian literature and politics. This was partly the result of greater cultural confidence, but it also reflected the anxiety of a sparsely populated country in an overcrowded world of superpowers. The movement has been beneficial in that it has contributed to an awakened sense of national purpose, but it is not without its attendant dangers. One extreme, concerned with the preservation of national characteristics, rejects any hint of outside influence; the other, eager to see Canada in the vanguard, attempts to jump on to the latest bandwagon (whatever its origins). This is in fact the contemporary version of the 'native' versus 'cosmopolitan' controversy that, as we shall see, raged in the 1920s. Both extremes, it is fair to assert, are excessive in their reactions; the former leads to an inbred stagnation, the latter to a sterile rootlessness. Moreover, in practice both seem to emphasize a particular kind of cultural alignment, the first harking back to British assumptions, the second tending to reflect modern American attitudes. A middle way is possible, however, and I hope that this book will show how, with varying degrees of success in different periods, this alternative road has been followed in the past.

Yet this is a feature of our literary history that has not yet been sufficiently acknowledged. Too much has been written about our 'colonial' literary deference. To be sure, early writers took a considerable time to realize that the conventions (and often the nuances of language) of the Old World were not, as they stood, the most precise instruments through which to explore and interpret the New. Similarly, our lesser writers slavishly imitated their betters, but this is not a peculiarly 'colonial' characteristic – it is equally true of their mediocre confrères in Britain and the

United States. It is more important to realize that, somewhat slowly but none the less surely, the truly talented Canadian writers found means to convey what W. W. E. Ross, in his verse-prologue to *Laconics* (1930), was to call 'the sharper tang of Canada'. Instances will multiply in later chapters, but a few samples may be offered here. Thus James Reaney's River Avon, in the first of his *Twelve Letters to a Small Town* (1962), has an imported name but it does not 'flow with English accents.' At times, of course, this distinction can be a liability. Hugh MacLennan has told how his literary agent in the United States had difficulty in placing his work because it seemed neither British nor American and was therefore regarded with distrust. The ideal blend may well remain elusive, but in 'Astrolabe', a poem published in *Something Still to Find* (1982), Douglas LePan asserted its attainability when speaking of 'this new world, ours, where savagery and sweetness melt as one'. This is, to be sure, an insecure as well as a perilous balance, but it has been maintained in the past and there is no intrinsic reason why it should not be maintained in the future.

Although it is no longer necessary to apologize for the quality of Canadian literature or even to argue for its existence, there are a number of other critical myths which need to be challenged: that our literature is too 'genteel' and tends to reflect bourgeois assumptions; that it avoids certain embarrassing subjects (exploitation of the native peoples, for example); that puritanism is still an inhibiting presence; that Canada is a cultural wasteland. All these charges had some validity in the past, even in the not-too-distant past, but they are no longer applicable to the literary decades that have produced (among others) Leonard Cohen, Robert Kroetsch, Margaret Laurence, Irving Layton, Alice Munro, Al Purdy, and Rudy Wiebe. Ironically, it is the effectiveness of certain Canadian texts – including Sinclair Ross's *As For Me and My House*, Layton's poems, and Laurence's Manawaka novels – that have tended to perpetuate these myths while they were in fact challenging and helping to deny their reality. Perhaps because Canadian criticism has emphasized literary themes rather than the writers' approaches to their material, it has too often failed to realize that, by publicly identifying and discussing an attitude or an absurdity, Canadian poets and novelists have played their part in robbing these conventional stances of their force and even their credibility. The more historical emphasis attempted in subsequent chapters of this book should reveal the gradual changes and reformulations achieved by each literary generation.

So far I have emphasized the impact of the British and American traditions upon Canadian literature and the continuing struggle to create an independent way between these differing models. It would be a mistake, however, to assume that the outside influences upon Canadian writing are confined to literature in English. A number of other factors are involved. Thus the fact that Canada is a distinctively northern nation has had a palpable effect upon the nature of its literature, and Robertson Davies once remarked – in jest, of course, but the jest has a serious point behind it – that the two great Canadian dramatists are Chekhov and Ibsen (Cameron interview 34). Certainly, climatic elements have helped to encourage certain Scandinavian characteristics within our literature, and a more direct link has been forged by writers like Laura Salverson and Martha Ostenso. More recently, Jack Hodgins has observed that the Pacific coastline of British Columbia extends down to Gabriel García Márquez's Colombia, thus implying that the recent links with South American 'magic realism' have a partly geographical explanation. Moreover, as reference to Salverson and Ostenso reminds us, the contribution of immigrants from outside Britain and the United States has, especially in recent years, been considerable. Most conspicuous is the achievement of Jewish authors – especially A. M. Klein, Layton, and Mordecai Richler – who have injected a much-needed independence of viewpoint and vitality of language into Canadian writing. But others, too, have portrayed their own ethnic worlds (Wiebe's Mennonites, Austin Clarke's Barbadians, and, more recently, the East Indians of Rohinton Mistry and M. G. Vassanji come immediately to mind) and have thereby enriched the literary presentation of that (in the main) healthy diversity that makes up modern Canada.

At this point, however, readers (especially, perhaps, non-Canadian readers) are likely to be struck by the absence in the foregoing discussion of any detailed discussion of French-Canadian or Québécois literature. Surely, it will be said, the interrelations between the writing in Canada's two official languages must have been deep and far-reaching. Unfortunately, this has not been the case. When MacLennan named his first novel about French Canada *Two Solitudes*, he intended to draw attention to the extension of Rilke's phrase which he quoted at length in the epigraph:

Love consists in this,
that two solitudes protect,
and touch, and greet each other.

But the narrower conception expressed in the title itself has proved a more accurate description of the socio-political realities.

Both sides have been at fault. English Canadians have been both condescending and neglectful, while French Canadians, aware not only of their numerical minority but of the threat to their language in English-dominated North America, have resisted any contact that might possibly contaminate their own culture. The pattern of Canada's own half envious, half suspicious attitude towards the United States is here reproduced within the country itself and with additional linguistic complications. The two solitudes, then, are primarily cultural, and although in recent years writers like F. R. Scott, John Glassco, D. G. Jones, and Fred Cogswell have attempted through translation to draw the attention of English-speaking Canada to the riches of its French-language equivalent, the cross-cultural results have only recently begun to make themselves felt. In literary criticism, a few comparative studies have been attempted – between Frederick Philip Grove and Ringuet, Munro and Anne Hébert, Kroetsch and Hubert Aquin, for instance – but (even if we assume smooth relations on the political level) another generation will probably pass before we see a healthy and mutual interchange between the two literatures. At the present time, English- and French-Canadian writing are best discussed separately.

Finally, I should not perhaps proceed with a historically oriented critical survey of Canadian literature in English without considering, even questioning, the efficacy of such an undertaking. Since critical histories of British and American literature are relatively common and accepted without challenge, it may seem that the concept of a Canadian equivalent is in no need of defence. But there are special reasons why the Canadian case is possibly controversial. For example, John Metcalf has written: 'History has dictated that writing in English transcends national boundaries' (*Kicking* 156). In an age of jet travel and instant communications, are not our writers automatically authors, as well as citizens, of the world? As early as Matthew Arnold, for whom the idea of a Canadian or Australian literature represented the *reductio ad absurdum* of literary and linguistic fragmentation, questioning voices have been raised. Canadian writers as diverse as Grove, for whom a national art was a contradiction in terms, and Richler, who had no intention of being no more than a large frog in what he considered a small pond, have for very different reasons expressed a similar unease at being categorized within a confined national boundary.

True, there can be something limiting in such a concentration, and much Canadian criticism is weakened if not vitiated by a constricted, even parochial outlook. Canadian literature is clearly a unit within a series of larger structures, and we might well adapt one of Arnold's own *aperçus* and observe that he who knows only his Canadian literature knows little of that. It is also worth noting that Margaret Atwood, for instance, generally seen by Canadians alongside Laurence and Munro, will look decidedly different to Americans, who are more likely to see her within a context including, say, Anne Sexton and Sylvia Plath. But there is no reason to believe that the perspective of the larger context renders that of the smaller in any way invalid. Shakespeare, Racine, Goethe, Tolstoy belong properly to the whole world, yet they are in essence English, French, German, and Russian respectively, and are best understood within the setting of their own national literatures. Canada is a relatively young country in a world that has become smaller and more closely interconnected by developments in media and transportation. Yet, like other countries, it is a distinct entity, and remains so in part by virtue of its culture. A critical history of Canadian literature may therefore be accepted as proper and desirable so long as it is not regarded as the sole context for those considered within it.

One further warning must be registered. To what extent, it should be asked, can the nation's diversity of terrain, population, and local attitudes be subsumed under the deceptively straightforward word 'Canadian'? Canada is still, more than most countries, a combination of dramatically varied regions. The Maritimes, Newfoundland, Québec, Ontario, the prairies, British Columbia, the northern territories: all these distinctive areas can boast their own literary tradition. The process of western development, for instance, was accompanied – or, to be more precise, followed – by a literary equivalent that W. H. New, in a happy phrase transfixed in a book title, has called 'articulating west'. It was and is a gradual, by no means smooth, but decidedly necessary procedure.

Consistently, western writers and commentators have registered much the same kind of unease about eastern Canadian assumptions that easterners have registered about British or American influences. Ontario took a long time to realize that it was no longer Canada West, and there is now more than one Canada West, as any journey between Alberta and British Columbia will demonstrate. In consequence, every Canadian may be said to possess at least two loyalties that are not always easily reconcilable: one to the country, one to the local region (not necessarily a province). We return once more to the basic awareness that Canada is a loose confederation of political and geographical units, often at odds with one another but still united, somewhat reluctantly, in a common purpose that at times may seem no more than a common solitude. For those who speak English, the language, moulded through two centuries into a distinctive accent and idiom, provides over the vast distances a medium through which this solitude can be explored, articulated, recognized as one's own. While no longer British, it is not in the accepted sense American. And so 'Canadian' emerges as a unique designation, and Canadian literature gradually, obstinately, impressively, forms itself as the embodiment of a scattered and elusive people's communal vision.

Part One

Early Stages

Chapter 1

The Beginnings in Prose

Paradoxically but appropriately, we detect the first clear signs of literary activity in English Canada in the work of travellers and explorers – paradoxically because they would not have considered themselves contributors to literature, appropriately because their efforts at surveying the terrain, describing both physical features and native inhabitants, were necessary first steps towards coming to terms, imaginatively as well as practically, with the country as a whole. Their prime motive was always utilitarian: establishing communications to improve the fur trade; investigating the viability of new routes by land or water; filling in the unknown spaces on early maps. Most of them originally came from abroad and eventually returned home; their reports were generally published in Europe either as contributions to scientific knowledge or as accounts of exciting travels in strange foreign lands. While some could offer little more than notes and diary jottings, others recorded their findings in the 'plain and unadorned Style', as Samuel Hearne described it in the dedication to his *Journey to the Northern Ocean,* which had become the eighteenth-century prose norm. A few, including George Vancouver and Simon Fraser, have given their names to parts of the country and so have achieved a vicarious personal immortality; others failed or neglected to preserve a permanent record of their adventures, and have passed into oblivion. And some – notably Hearne, Alexander Mackenzie, and David Thompson – helped indirectly but palpably to initiate a Canadian literary tradition.

Alexander Henry – usually designated 'the elder' to distinguish him from his fur-trading nephew of the same name – published his *Travels and Adventures in Canada and the Indian Territories* in 1809. His literary-historical importance is to some extent accidental. In 1763 he was one of the few survivors of Pontiac's sacking of Fort Michilimackinac, an event that was to provide a gory climax to John Richardson's melodramatic but influential novel *Wacousta* (1832). Furthermore, his account so impressed Anna Jameson at the outset of her Canadian travels that, in her own words, it 'had some influence in directing the course of my present tour' (*Winter Studies* III 17). But Henry is important for other reasons. The account of his adventures, apparently accurate in the main though much of it reads suspiciously like fiction, bears witness to his ready adaptability to new ways. En route to Michilimackinac he disguised himself as a Canadian because of Indian hostility to the English at that time, and later passed himself off as an Indian to escape being killed after the massacre. Claiming to have become 'as expert in the Indian pursuits [hunting beaver and raccoon], as the Indians themselves' (Ch. 15), he is a dramatic example of the need to change habits and preconceptions in order to come to terms with life in the New World. Above all, he writes in a clear, unostentatious, flowing English prose – 'plain, unaffected, telling what he has to tell in few and simple words, and without comment', as Jameson says (III 17) – that offers an admirable model, not always followed, for later prose writers.

Samuel Hearne led three expeditions between 1769 and 1772 to investigate Indian stories about rich copper deposits in the northern wilds, succeeded at the third attempt, and became the first white man to cross the Barren Lands and reach the Arctic Ocean. His adventures, published in 1795, make up an absorbing narrative rightly famous for its description of the massacre of a small group of Inuit by Hearne's party of Indians. The importance of this incident derives from Hearne's realization that he is helpless to prevent the slaughter (all he can do is exhort them to be mercifully quick in their killing), that the human sentiments he has brought with him from Europe are not shared by the guides on whom he is dependent, and that the new world in which he finds himself bears no resemblance, either physical or moral, to his own. Hearne on the Coppermine River is a Gulliver-like castaway in a world turned upside down. His ostensible discovery – that the deposits are poor in quality and the river unsuitable for navigation – is trivial compared with his insight into the savagery of unaccommodated man in the northern wilderness. When a young Inuit girl is being murdered at his feet, he is torn between sympathy for the victim, disgust at her assailants, and horror at the precariousness of his own situation. The account is all the more moving in being communicated through Hearne's incongruously rational eighteenth-century prose; it becomes a symbolic moment for modern humanity.

By contrast, Alexander Mackenzie presents himself as eighteenth-century man bringing his own standards of scientific investigation into a new environment. While Hearne's account is a narrative, Mackenzie's is more like an official report. His book is entitled *Voyages from Montreal on the River St. Laurence Through the Continent of North America to the Frozen and Pacific Oceans in the Years 1789 and 1793* (1801). The story of his inscribing the message 'Alexander Mackenzie, from Canada, by land, the twenty-second of July, one thousand seven-hundred and ninety-three' on a rock overlooking the Pacific is well known; but even more impressive is the fact that he accomplished the feat in the threatening presence of strange Indians of whom his guides were afraid. Not only this, but according to his own testimony he calmly took his meridian – 'I would not stir till I had accomplished my object' (*Journals and Letters* 378) – and so created another symbolic moment that balances Hearne's. Both his book and his journals are full of information for the geographer, geologist, historian, and anthropologist, but it is at moments such as these that the accounts of the explorers impinge upon the literary imagination.

Of all the explorers of North America, however, the greatest was probably David Thompson. Not only did he investigate and map vast stretches of hitherto unknown territory, but he brought an intellectually disciplined and scientifically inquisitive approach to the whole process of exploration and discovery. Unfortunately, his papers were not published in full until over fifty years after his death, and although his achievements are now recognized by scholars and scientists, they failed to create the imaginative impact that might have been expected. The findings of all these explorers (and many more) were of practical use in their own time and remain of historical importance. In recent years these struggles and accomplishments have been re-created by modern poets, examples including Don Gutteridge's *Coppermine*, John Newlove's 'Samuel Hearne in Wintertime', and the passages derived from Thompson in Newlove's best-known poem 'The Pride'. Gradually, then, their achievements are being incorporated into the Canadian literary experience.

As we might expect, the first consciously literary works to be produced in what is now Canada originated in the Maritimes, where the early settlers had been joined after 1783 by an influx of Loyalists from the 'rebel colonies' then in process of transforming themselves into the United States. Here was the nucleus for a distinctive society, and it was not long before writing that surveyed, analyzed, and often satirized this emergent society began to appear in print. In his own time, the most distinguished literary figure in the Maritimes was considered to be Joseph Howe, and his 'Western and Eastern Rambles', contributed to the *Novascotian* between 1828 and 1831, are useful if excessively rhetorical and flippant accounts of his travels within the colony. Most of his other writings, however, are of interest less to the literary critic than to the student of Maritime history and politics. Of more lasting importance for the evolution of a characteristically Canadian literature is the work of Thomas McCulloch and T. C. Haliburton.

McCulloch's literary significance has only become clear in comparatively recent years. Late in 1821 a series of letters purporting to describe the life and manners of an unnamed Nova Scotian town began to appear in the *Acadian Recorder* under an obvious pseudonym. The author was soon identified as the Presbyterian principal of Pictou Academy, though it was not until after McCulloch's death that the material appeared as a book, *The Letters of Mephibosheth Stepsure* (1862). Even then it attracted little attention, and realization of its quality had to await republication for a wider audience as *The Stepsure Letters* in 1960.

In retrospect, one of the most significant characteristics of the *Letters* is the fact that they were written primarily for a local readership. McCulloch had hoped to send 'the whole home [to Scotland] as a sample of the way in which we get on in the western world' (1960 ed. 157), but the plan never materialized, and in any case the local preoccupation is insisted upon within the text itself. McCulloch was writing it in a Halifax weekly, and his concern was to draw the attention of the colonial capital to the small enclosed communities in the rural areas. 'Chronicles of our town' becomes a recurrent phrase. The *Letters* represent, in fact, the first manifestation in our literature of a Canadian small town, and the contrast between rural and urban patterns of life, between small town and metropolis (often with a satiric edge to the writing), becomes a fruitful subject extending through Haliburton to Leacock and beyond. That McCulloch anticipates Leacock in having a 'Rev. Mr Drone' as his local minister may perhaps be attributed to coincidence, but it could represent an early example of the continuities of cultural tradition.

The *Letters* paint a humorous and often critical portrait of an isolated Maritime community. They begin with an account of a number of enforced guests in the sheriff's house whose stories provide cautionary tales on the results of idleness, excessive ambition, and dissipation. Later, Stepsure offers his own story and presents himself as a modest, obedient, hard-working young man who succeeds by practising all the official virtues and especially by espousing 'industry, domestic comfort, and religion' (Letter 14). The Scots' love of garrulous and rather wordy humour is evident throughout, and McCulloch has much fun with comic names such as Mr Soakem the tavern-keeper, Mr Snout the pig-farmer, and Tubal Thump the blacksmith. There is also more than a trace of the down-to-earth Swiftian eighteenth century in McCulloch; at one point his critic 'Censor' is made to soar 'feet foremost into Peg's [Pegasus's] huge accumulation of odoriferous sweets' (Letter 18). The letters begin uncertainly – mainly, I suspect, because a central focus is lacking. They improve as soon as Stepsure concentrates on himself and firmly establishes his stance as the complacently upright narrator. Above all, the reader readily accepts Stepsure's town as an authentic community; the sense of bustling reality persuades us that more people inhabit the place than are actually mentioned. Moreover, the characters who appear would, if sufficiently developed, become convincing participants in a novel that never in fact materializes. By no stretch of the imagination could McCulloch be described as a major writer, but he demonstrates his capacity to create a fictive world.

McCulloch's intentions are thoroughly didactic, but he is a firm believer in the sugared pill and creates a medium in which we are prepared to accept his moral lay sermons. His techniques can be complex. Thus Stepsure uses Drone in the same way that McCulloch uses Stepsure, to provide advice that is at the same time distanced and rendered palatable through humour. Though constant reference is made to the congregation sleeping through Drone's sermons, his moral position generally carries McCulloch's implicit support. Similarly, McCulloch pokes fun at Stepsure's self-complacency and the alacrity with which he criticizes his neighbours. Thus when Stepsure complains of his neighbour Trot's 'habit of thinking and talking about folks' business' (Letter 13), we realize that the words apply equally well to Stepsure himself. At the same time McCulloch employs Stepsure throughout as the purveyor of a practical, homespun wisdom. The effects that McCulloch develops in presenting his narrator are surprisingly sophisticated; one comes to wonder, indeed, whether the 'Censor' who writes pious attacks on Stepsure in the *Recorder* and is duly answered therein may not be another McCulloch persona. It is worth noting that Robertson Davies, himself heir to the Canadian satirical tradition initiated here, has gone so far as to praise the book as 'a finer piece of Canadian irony than the much-praised Sam Slick stories of Judge Haliburton' (*Well-Tempered* 235).

While Thomas Chandler Haliburton shared many of McCulloch's subjects for satire, notably the alleged idleness and passivity of Nova Scotians, his techniques were very different and decidedly more ambitious. Stepsure was a native exposing local shortcomings to his fellows, but in *The Clockmaker* (three series, 1836–40) Nova Scotia and its people are subjected to the scrutiny of outsiders – Sam Slick the Yankee pedlar and a visiting English 'Squire'. The 'Bluenoses', then, are presented in their colonial situation from the viewpoints of representatives of the two nations that most dominate them. This conception soon bursts the bounds of Haliburton's original intention, however, and he extends the range of his satire to make fun of the Americans and the English as well. After the first two series, in which Sam takes the Squire on various 'circuits' around Nova Scotia (once again contrasting with the sedentary Stepsure), the two visit New England, at which time Haliburton, presumably wishing to reverse the effect and present a colonial confronting American manners and mores, coolly but inconsistently proclaims the Squire a native of Nova Scotia. Then, finding that the public is still eager for more of Sam Slick, he packs both of them off to England so that Yankee and Nova Scotian can observe John Bull on his home ground in *The Attaché* (1843–4). The Squire, now named Thomas Poker, acts throughout as a mask for Haliburton himself who becomes, as it were, a stooge to his original creation, the irrepressible clockmaker.

Haliburton, a Loyalist descendant with a conservative philosophy and a deep distrust of the United States, nevertheless admired the energy and practicality so prominent in the American character. He was determined to encourage the development of Nova Scotia (especially the construction of railways and canals to stimulate trade), and felt that vigorous methods were required. 'Those Bluenoses won't try what they can do', complains Sam; they must be 'shamed' into exerting themselves (First

Series, Ch. 12). At the same time, Haliburton wishes to warn Nova Scotians against the levelling, republican attitudes from south of the border. Sam is therefore a complex character, whose opinions sometimes carry conviction but are sometimes to be condemned. Like McCulloch, Haliburton offers lay sermons and comic parables, the didactic pill sugared with puns, tall tales, and farcical inventions. Sam is continually recalling stories that point useful morals, and when the latter are approved by Haliburton they are printed in conspicuous italics. Although his message is now understandably outdated, the sketches are not, mainly because of Haliburton's verbal expertise in reproducing Sam's inimitable voice.

The language is vigorous, colloquial, often ungrammatical, anything but 'correct'. Sam becomes, indeed, a veritable symbol of the American impact upon Canadian literature from the earliest times. The so-called gentility of the British influence is immediately challenged, but – and this is a crucial qualification – Sam's speech depends for its effectiveness on the formal rules that he breaks with such evident relish. The standard English represented by the Squire provides the frame, even perhaps the norm, against which Sam's irrepressible dialect can be measured. Many of his proverbial sayings have passed into the language – not just the Canadian language but English as it is spoken throughout the world. Such everyday phrases and sayings as 'upper crust', 'as large as life and twice as natural', and 'a nod is as good as a wink' originate with Haliburton – or, rather, with Sam Slick.

This speech is, of course, a literary convention, and those who complain about Haliburton's mixture of Yankee dialect and characteristics with those of western frontiersmen miss the creative element within his work. One commentator detects as early as the first series of *The Clockmaker* 'the friction between precept and example' (Davies ed. 249), and the increased interest that Haliburton displays in narration for its own sake (another manifestation of this creative impulse) becomes especially evident in *The Old Judge* (1849), a collection of sketches that desert Sam Slick but concentrate once again on Nova Scotia. Subtitled 'Life in a Colony', it consists of a varied set of descriptions, arguments, and short stories all illustrating Nova Scotian life at an earlier period. One of the first works in Canadian literature to look back in nostalgia to an earlier period in the country's development, it follows such popular writers as Washington Irving in the United States and Mary Russell Mitford in

England in providing a valuable picture of the customs and practices of a past age. The collection is unified not only by the regional emphasis but by a complex series of narrators who are as illustrative as the tales they tell. Thus the five chapters with the general title 'The Keeping-Room of an Inn' offer in Stephen Richardson, 'one of the oddest fellows in the country' and 'a regular character' (Ch. 11), a spokesman who can rival Sam Slick while at the same time manifesting a remarkable modern consciousness of the artifice of fiction. The book opens with the hilarious 'How Many Fins Has a Cod?' and all but ends with 'The Witch of Inky Dell', a supernatural story worthy to rank with Sir Walter Scott's 'Wandering Willie's Tale'. Though Haliburton's true medium was imaginative non-fiction, his skill in short fiction was considerable, and any anthology of Canadian short stories should begin with specimens of his work.

While Nova Scotia was developing a sense of community that could be explored through the comparatively sophisticated medium of satire, Ontario was still being cleared and settled by pioneers, and the earliest literature of permanent interest from what was then Upper Canada portrayed the challenge and impact of the pioneering experience. The dominant or at least dominating figure was William 'Tiger' Dunlop, so called from his original method of killing tigers, which consisted (at least in legend) of throwing snuff in their faces and shooting them while they were still confused. When Dunlop came to Canada from Britain, he was already an established member of the literary circle centred upon *Blackwood's Magazine*. An inveterate anecdotalist, renowned drinker, and unflinching enthusiast for the pioneering life, he wrote energetically and amusingly, although one gets the impression from his improbably titled *Statistical Sketches of Upper Canada* (1832) and his *Recollections of the American War, 1812–1814* (serialized 1847) that he was more impressive in the flesh than on the page. Nevertheless, his bluff vigour often shows through his writing: 'If there were in nature (which is doubtful) such a being as a sober blacksmith, he might make a fortune' (*Statistical*, Ch. 1); 'it would perhaps be too much, to expect people to practise as well as to preach Christian charity' (Ch. 9). His forcefulness needs to be stressed as a balance to the better known, more genteel accounts of pioneering life by the Strickland sisters, Catharine Parr Traill and Susanna Moodie.

For reasons of biography and convenience, Traill and Moodie are generally treated together. Both married half-pay officers and emigrated to Canada in 1832 (the year of Dunlop's *Statistical Sketches*) to take up land. They came from the gentry class, but the family fortunes were declining, and both had achieved a modest financial as well as literary success as authors while still in England. Both settled near Peterborough, and had at first to endure primitive conditions for which they were ill prepared. Both wrote literary accounts of their experiences addressed specifically to an English readership. There, however, the resemblances cease, and their writings have a particular interest because the two sisters, though alike in situation, were totally opposed in temperament.

Traill wrote children's fiction, guidebooks, and works of natural history, but is best known for *The Backwoods of Canada* (1836), an account of her first years in the New World written in epistolary form and probably modelled on Gilbert White's *The Natural History of Selborne*. This form allows her not only to describe the pioneering experience but to re-create the complex and often painful process of change and adjustment. The letters are written to her mother, relatives, and friends, and allow her to relay information, pursue her personal interests, and chronicle her response to her new environment. Internal evidence makes it clear that they have been adapted for literary effect, and that her apparent simplicity and directness of style depend upon the art that conceals art.

She is remarkable for her intelligence, cheerfulness of demeanour, and openness to new experiences. 'It has ever been my way' she records, 'to extract the sweet rather the bitter in the cup of life ... Since we are here, let us make the best of it' (Letter 18). As a result, she refers lightheartedly to 'our Robinson Crusoe sort of life', and both acknowledges and accepts the incongruity of her situation by referring to 'we *bush-settlers*' (Letters 8, 15). She is careful to insist that the emigrant should 'discard every thing exclusively pertaining to the artificial refinements of fashionable life in England' and notes that 'it is education and manners that must distinguish the gentleman in this country' (Introduction; Letter 6). She does not abandon the true standards of civilization that she has left behind; rather, she rejects what no longer matters while retaining the principles of decency and good sense that she accepts as universally valid.

The Backwoods, like her later *Female Emigrant's Guide* (1854), deliberately caters to women settlers, since most other accounts (including Dunlop's) were written by men for men, although 'the hardships and difficulties of the settler's life ... are felt peculiarly by the female part of the family' (Introduction). But the interest of the book transcends any possible limitation of sex. She is concerned not only with the day-to-day trials of early pioneers but with deeper and more permanent issues involved in settling a new land. Thus, like many immigrants from Europe, she laments the absence of any material sense of a historical past, but her eye for beauty and her enthusiasm for natural history (some of her best chapters are devoted to animals, birds, and especially flowers) find ample compensation for this deficiency. Her book is packed full of information and shrewd commentary, but the controlling factor is always the calm, attractive, interesting-because-always-interested personality of the writer. 'To me nothing that bears the stamp of novelty is devoid of interest', she writes (Letter 4), and although she inevitably imports many of the preconceptions of her class, she never flaunts them as her sister so often does. Where Moodie, for instance, devotes pages of outraged superiority to the uncouthness of her American neighbours, Traill merely refers in passing to 'the annoying Yankee manners that distinguish many of the earlier-settled townships' (Letter 15). Unruffled and unassuming, she treats herself almost as an external character, observed like everyone else, while Moodie is always conspicuously at the centre of her narrative.

Traill deliberately eschewed the fictional mode in *The Backwoods* and asserted that 'the simple truth, founded entirely on personal knowledge of the facts related, is the basis of the work' (Introduction). Despite similar assertions of accuracy, Moodie never adhered to so rigid a principle. She could not resist altering and heightening her material. The essential difference in approach between the sisters can readily be illustrated by the opening pages of their books. Traill begins with a clear and straightforward account of the departure of herself and her husband from Greenock and a description of the ship in which they sailed. Moodie opens *Roughing It in the Bush* (1852) with the statement: 'The dreadful cholera was depopulating Quebec and Montreal.' Not only are we immediately introduced to a situation of crisis and danger, but we are simultaneously aware of a writer intent on controlling and transforming her subject. She was not herself afflicted by the epidemic – ironically it was Traill who almost succumbed to the disease and described the course of her illness briefly and without fuss. Characteristically, Moodie wishes to play up the dramatic possibilities of the situation. Similarly, when the health officials come aboard we are presented not with credible, realistically drawn individuals but with emblems of Moodie's prejudices concerning the typical inhabitants of Upper and Lower Canada. When a Bible is needed upon which to swear an oath, and Moodie offers (of all things) a volume of Voltaire as a substitute, we can see that we are in the presence of a writer more interested in symbolic effect than documentary verisimilitude.

Like Haliburton's *The Old Judge, Roughing It in the Bush* is a miscellany made up of personal impressions, character sketches, passages of romantic description, anecdotes, short stories, and even poems. The switch from tone to tone is frequently abrupt, and it is a mistake to accept all her statements at face value. Moodie is a difficult writer to come to terms with because she can so easily be either over- or under-rated. Stylistically she is often rough and crude, her reasoning often conventional and trite. All her effects are heightened (it is worth remembering that she grew up in a period when melodrama was an accepted literary mode), and it is not always easy to decide whether they are deliberate or unconscious. On the other hand, the extent of her humour and self-parody can readily be underestimated. At the beginning of the book she seems to go out of her way to present herself as even more helpless than she initially was in order to exaggerate the force of her conversion by the end. There is often a slapstick absurdity about the events portrayed, and one detects a hilarity dangerously close to hysteria.

Indeed, while reading Moodie we frequently receive painful glimpses of a mind at the end of its tether. 'Brian the Still-Hunter', for instance, purports to be an account of a fellow immigrant known to the Moodies. Part of his story is offered as what would now be called black humour; at one point, he tries while on a boating expedition to commit suicide by cutting his throat, and his rescuer threatens: 'If you dare to try that again, I will kill you with the oar.' Later, he himself tells an unlikely story about a stag attacked by wolves in order to raise the question 'Is God just to his creatures?' In terms of realism, all this seems incredible. One suspects, however, that Brian has been introduced to communicate responses to the bush that Moodie could not present in her own person. A respectable English gentlewoman could hardly admit to thoughts of suicide herself, nor could the questioning of God's justice be offered by one who elsewhere reproduces the standard Christian pieties. Brian is unconvincing as a realistically conceived character but fascinating as a psychological projection; there but for the grace of God, we feel, goes Susanna Moodie.

Moodie wrote many novels and poems, though none of these has gained the continuing interest of modern readers. Her sequel to *Roughing It, Life in the Clearings* (1853), repeats the miscellany formula, but the material is less original and less interesting, and her attempt to weld it into a whole by the stale device of a trip to Niagara Falls is perfunctory in the extreme. Her reputation rests, then, upon this awkward, angular book existing (like so much of Haliburton) in the curious middle ground between fiction and non-fiction. If we value consistency of attitude and control of tone, Traill is by far the more rewarding writer. But Moodie, for all her faults, manages – albeit in hit-or-miss fashion – to present a remarkably compelling picture of the psychological tensions that must have characterized many of the immigrants of her time. While Traill has more in common with the late eighteenth century and the Regency of Jane Austen, Moodie recalls the roughcast literary world of R. S. Surtees and the Irish anecdotalists like William Carleton and Charles Lever, the world that the young Dickens entered but soon transcended. Yet the miscellany proved a surprisingly useful medium for Moodie's purpose; in the crude pioneering context her lack of polish seems right, and she was able to maintain a precarious balance between the cogent and the absurd that reflected something in her environment that her sister's more disciplined literary gifts were unable to catch. She is a provokingly uneven writer but, as Margaret Atwood's poem-cycle *The Journals of Susanna Moodie* testifies, she continues to haunt the Canadian literary consciousness.

Hard upon the heels of the settlers came the tourist-travellers. Indeed, Anna Jameson had arrived in Canada while Traill and Moodie were still establishing themselves in the bush, and *Winter Studies and Summer Rambles* (1838), though an outsider's view, provides an impression of early Canada that can be obtained nowhere else. Jameson moved in high social, intellectual, and literary circles in England, and brought to her exploratory tour of Canada the wit and poise of an accomplished professional writer. In her good-humoured acceptance of new experiences she is closer to Traill than to Moodie, but she is less self-effacing than the former and far more balanced in her judgements than the latter. Her winter was based in Toronto, likened to 'a fourth or fifth rate provincial town, with the pretensions of a capital city' (I 98), and her summer rambles took her through southwestern Ontario and up Lake Huron to visit Indian settlements. She responds to the scenic splendour of the country through which she passes, but does not neglect to mention the rattlesnakes and mosquitoes. Moreover, she can assimilate both beauties and hardships within a prose that moves smoothly between extremes without drawing undue attention to itself. Her range is remarkable. At one moment she is lamenting the murderous instincts of human beings: 'thus we repaid the beauty, and enjoyment, and lavish loveliness spread around us, with pain and with destruction' (III 331). At another she insists on running the rapids with an Indian guide, and drily comments: 'I recommend it as an exercise before breakfast' (III 200). One of Jameson's charms is that, while offering a thoughtful and just account of her travels, she takes neither the country nor herself too seriously. As a result, *Winter Studies and Summer Rambles* (apart from the extended, unintegrated, and dry discussions of German scholarship) is both informative and refreshing.

As Canada began to take shape in the second half of the nineteenth century, travel literature became a prominent form of non-fiction, though no indisputable masterpiece of the genre appeared. Paul Kane's *Wanderings of an Artist among the Indians of North America* (1859) deserves mention for its predominantly aesthetic rather than practical response to the scenery of central and western Canada and for its valuable juxtaposition of records in verbal and pictorial form. Politically motivated travel books were also produced, notable among these being William Francis Butler's *The Great Lone Land* (1872) and G. M. Grant's *Ocean to Ocean* (1873). Lieutenant Butler was loosely connected with the Wolseley expedition dispatched to Red River at the time of the first Riel rebellion, and was later sent by the Canadian government into what is now Saskatchewan and Alberta to inquire into the extent of contemporary smallpox epidemics among the Indians and to gather information about the maintenance of law and order in the west. His book begins flippantly as the lighthearted account of a soldier-adventurer, but the country and the native inhabitants impressed Butler, and it ends as the eloquent and sympathetic record of a four-month journey that vividly evokes a still unsettled land.

Butler, of course, was yet another visitor who came and went, but in

Ocean to Ocean G. M. Grant, later to become an influential principal of Queen's University, produced the first native travel-book of any consequence. Subtitled 'Sir Sandford Fleming's Expedition through Canada in 1872', it arose out of a surveying party appointed to determine the best route for the Canadian Pacific Railway. Like *The Great Lone Land* it offers an ostensibly lighthearted approach influenced more, one suspects, by Victorian taste in humour than by any attempt to imitate Jameson's stylistic high spirits. Grant aimed to 'find out something about the real extent and resources of our Dominion' (Ch. 13), and a sense of expansionist confidence pervades the book; but Grant also communicates 'a genuine love for camp life, for its freedom and simplicity and rude happiness, for the earth as a couch and the sky for a canopy, and the wide world for a bed-room' (Ch. 10), a strain often evoked in subsequent Canadian writing in both prose and verse, but rarely so endearingly as here. It is pleasantly, indeed artfully written, and deserves its reputation as a minor classic.

Many of the qualities found sporadically in early Canadian prose – humorous didacticism, an ironic view of small communities, non-fiction on the verge of fiction, the genial rhythms of a personal voice – come together in the work of Stephen Leacock. Leacock is, of course, universally known as a humorist, but a surprising amount of his work has a serious motive. I am not merely thinking of his separate books on political science, education, and social questions (the products of Professor Leacock of McGill), nor of the profundity said to underlie all humour worthy of the name. I refer rather to the existence, within his humorous collections, of essays and sections intended to be more than just funny. Among his characteristically alliterative titles, it is worth noting, we find not only *Further Foolishness* (1916) but *Winnowed Wisdom* (1926), and Leacock is continually juxtaposing the two qualities. *Further Foolishness* unexpectedly contains a whole section entitled 'Peace, War, and Politics', while *Winnowed Wisdom* offers typically Leacockian subjects like 'The Cross-word Puzzle Craze' and 'At the Ladies' Culture Club' alongside other sketches which, though humorous in treatment, have solemn titles like 'The Next War'. In general, it is true to say that he is at his best when wisdom grows naturally out of his humour, unsuccessful when we suspect that he has merely grafted wisdom on to the humorous.

Leacock's work can conveniently be divided into three kinds. The wholly serious writings need not detain us long; they usually arose out of particular historical circumstances – world war, economic depression, etc. – and what Leacock had to say rarely transcended the occasion on which he said it. On the other hand, his short comic pieces, playing upon universal human qualities, both parodying and upholding the attitudes and responses of the average person, often display his gifts at their best. They raise a special critical problem, however. 'My Financial Career', the opening sketch in his first humorous book, *Literary Lapses* (1910), is invariably praised, perhaps because it was the first of its kind and displays a freshness that cannot be re-created. Leacock's commercially profitable habit of gathering his sketches annually to catch the Christmas sales – did a long-term disservice to his art. Not only did it result in the preservation of inferior material, but it encouraged the consecutive and concentrated reading of work that is most effective in small doses. The majority of his books are accumulations rather than organic wholes. It is no coincidence that his most successful, *Sunshine Sketches of a Little Town* and *Arcadian Adventures with the Idle Rich,* are both unified by a common locale and recurring characters, and that a continuing comic *invention* (as distinct from a series of discrete comic routines) is maintained throughout.

Sunshine Sketches (1912) was well categorized by Hugh Hood as 'a pastoral idyll treated satirically' (Struthers interview 26–7), and the mixture of probing satire and warm nostalgia is a conspicuous feature of his work. He is often at his best when he allows himself to 'turn on the gramophone of recollection' (*My Remarkable Uncle,* 'The British Soldier'), and Mariposa has become famous as the archetypal Canadian 'little Town in the Sunshine that once we knew' (*Sunshine Sketches,* 'L'Envoi'). Much of *Sunshine Sketches* is, indeed, pure fun, and reverse-situation humour is common. Thus the lifeboats of the *Mariposa Belle* sink and their occupants have to be rescued by the stricken ship; Josh Smith's efforts at the church fire are directed towards increasing the destruction rather than stopping it; Peter Pupkin is ashamed to acknowledge his parents because they are too rich rather than too poor. But Leacock's ultimate effect is more complex than his title suggests, and is achieved in part by his careful choice of a narrator who is both a native Mariposan and one who has known life in the big city. We can thus recognize both the parochiality and universality of the town; it is different from everywhere else, yet essentially the same. Leacock's two poles are the small town and the metropolis, and this is, in a sense, his version of Swift's Lilliput and Brobdingnag: what is shocking and threatening when magnified in Plutoria (as Leacock demonstrates in the ironically titled *Arcadian Adventures*) is charmingly absurd on a small scale. Commentators have often remarked that, under the superficial geniality of *Sunshine Sketches*, Mariposa is shown to be corrupt, petty, and hypocritical – worse, that it apes the very values of the metropolis it claims to reject. But the effect of the book depends upon Leacock's ability to persuade us to hold two apparently opposed attitudes in balance; we look at Mariposa critically, but also with love.

Arcadian Adventures (1914) is similar in subject but very different in tone. The same topics – financial speculation, romantic love, church politics, elections – are treated again, but this time bitter indignation is discernible behind the writing. Savage satire replaces the gentle, poised irony of the earlier book. *Sunshine Sketches* is, basically, about 'us'; *Arcadian Adventures* is about 'them'. This is not just a matter of the former being set in Canada and the latter in the United States (though the distinction is present, and reflects a suspicion prominent in Canadian culture from the Loyalists to the present day). Ultimately, it is an artistic difference, an effect of narrative control and perspective. While the relation between narrator and reader in *Sunshine Sketches* involves the sharing of a poignant memory, in *Arcadian Adventures* it is a mordant recognition of a world we perforce inhabit but cannot change. Nevertheless, both books are alike in displaying a sustained inventive creativity that goes far beyond what Leacock accomplished elsewhere.

Like most writers who achieve a lasting reputation, Leacock is remarkable for a well-defined style, a personal voice, and a fastidious concern for words. He makes fun not only of human institutions and frailties but of fictional techniques (*Nonsense Novels, Frenzied Fiction*) and our ways of using and abusing language. He has a particularly keen ear for the linguistically pretentious. In *Sunshine Sketches*, for example, he writes of the Mariposa undertaker: 'Mr Gingham had the true spirit of his profession, and such words as "funeral" or "coffin" or "hearse" never passed his lips. He spoke always of "interments", of "caskets", and "coaches"' ('The Hostelry of Mr Smith'). And in 'The Attaboy Language' (*Winnowed Wisdom*) he produces 'an attaboy dictionary' and translates specimens of Macaulay and Gibbon into contemporary slang. Above all, to quote Robertson Davies, who inherited from Leacock both humorous techniques and a concern for verbal directness, 'his best work has a pure magic rooted in speech' (*Stephen Leacock* 58). What comes off the page is a man talking, not an authority pontificating. His colloquial rhythms (which can embody the thoughtful and the moving) were not wholly new in Canada, as the writings of Haliburton, Jameson, and Sara Jeannette Duncan attest. But it was Leacock who helped to break down the more ponderous formalities of Victorian artistic convention, brought this intimate flexible prose to fruition, and made it available for subsequent writers.

Chapter 2

The Beginnings in Poetry

> Ye who, in stanzas, celebrate the Po,
> Or teach the Tyber in your streams to flow,
> How would you toil for numbers to proclaim
> The liquid grandeur of St. Lawrence' Stream?
>
> Go to – describe the indescribable,
>   And draw what never can be represented –
> Some subjects mock the painter's, poet's skill,
>   Feeble if written – feebler still if painted ...
> A THOMSON's almost all-descriptive pow'rs
> Might powerless fall before this theme of ours.

These are the opening lines, respectively, of J. MacKay's *Quebec Hill* (1797) and Arthur Slader's *The Burning City* (1837), an account of a disastrous fire in Saint John, New Brunswick. Both allude to – indeed, tend to demonstrate – a trend that became increasingly evident to poets in early Canada: that the language and metrical forms evolved over centuries to suit the needs of European life and literature were ill-equipped to convey the very different North American experience. What had been a problem for the explorer-adventurers (who could hide behind the persona of the ordinary non-literary man) and a frustration for the more articulate of the pioneer writers (both Traill and Moodie indirectly reveal the inadequacy of picturesque vocabulary for those living and working within the picture) became for the poets a crippling disablement. A sense of tradition may well be more important for a poet than for a writer in any other literary genre. There were, of course, the inevitable poetasters who readily churned out the same kind of pastoral, amatory, meditative, or religious verse that was being produced by their counterparts in 'the old country', but whenever writers like MacKay and Slader tackled ambitious subjects involving the particularities of their own world, statements about the difficulty or impossibility of finding an appropriate style seemed sure to follow.

As might be expected, much early poetry written in what is now Canada retains only historical as distinct from literary importance. The first Canadian poem of any consequence and substance is, in my view, Oliver Goldsmith's *The Rising Village* (1825, rev. 1834), and its special interest derives in part from a coincidence that enabled its author both to follow English poetic tradition and to adapt it to his own purpose. The Oliver Goldsmith in question (who was born in St. Andrews, New Brunswick, as the son of a Loyalist official, lived in Halifax, and worked as a colonial administrator) was the grandnephew of the Anglo-Irish Oliver Goldsmith, author of *The Deserted Village* (1770), and he found himself in a unique position to exploit the shared name. *The Deserted Village*, it may be remembered, ends with the dispossessed inhabitants of Auburn moving down to the ships that will take them to a virtually enforced exile. *The Rising Village* begins where the earlier poem left off, and traces on the opposite side of the Atlantic the growth of a new community from the ruins of the old. The emphasis is on growth rather than decay; the 'golden age' is located in the future rather than in the past.

The Canadian Goldsmith employs the same verse form as his ancestor (rhymed pentameter couplets), and alludes to the earlier poem either by means of brief quotation or through descriptions of church, inn, schoolmaster, village sports, etc., that relate in terms of comparison or contrast to equivalent passages in his formal model. Indeed, a principle of similarity within difference proves to be the poet's most important literary effect. On the one hand, similarity is established through subject matter, verse form, and language; on the other, he emphasizes the fact that, in the words of his grand-uncle's poem, 'these charms are fled' from England but are re-created (with adaptations) in Nova Scotia. This formal resemblance locates *The Rising Village* within a recognized cultural tradition, and the deliberate references back to the earlier poem absolve the Canadian Goldsmith from any charge of abject or unconscious imitation. He has created a structure of apparent imitation in which actual distinctions between 'Britannia' and 'Acadia' can be neatly registered. Unfortunately, he lacks the intellectual sharpness and clarity of his namesake. It is uncertain, for example, whether he fully comprehends – or, in the process of writing, remembers – the socio-political criticism of his grand-uncle. Thus, when he refers, in a passage praising British achievements, to 'The merchant's glory, and the farmer's pride' (l. 32), he seems to have forgotten the attacks on commercial luxury and opulence at the centre of the argument of *The Deserted Village;* and when the Nova Scotian villagers eventually drive the Indians from their native haunts just as their own people were forced into exile by the enclosing landowners of Britain, it is uncertain (to say the least) whether Goldsmith either intends or recognizes the irony.

Ultimately, however, it is the Canadian Goldsmith's slack rhythms and hand-me-down language that prevent him from matching the effect of his predecessor. He can produce clear, rather obviously balanced eighteenth-century couplets, but he cannot create the personal voice that speaks to us in *The Deserted Village.* The following descriptive lines are representative of the general standard:

> The farmer's village, bosomed 'mong the trees,
> Whose spreading branches shelter from the breeze;
> The winding stream that turns the busy mill,
> Whose clacking echos o'er the distant hill;
> The neat white church, beside whose walls are spread
> The grass-clod hillocks of the sacred dead ...
>
> (ll. 459–64)

This is serviceable, workmanlike verse, but little more; the conventional phrases, expected adjectives, and predictable rhymes indicate that Goldsmith could never have been an unequivocal pioneer in Canadian poetry. He was unable to dominate words and control metrical effects in the manner of his grand-uncle; his was not a new voice, and his subject required a new voice. *The Rising Village* lacks the verbal subtlety, rhythmic range, and variety of tone that distinguished its model. Nevertheless, the creative use the author makes of his ancestor's work renders it of far greater interest than later presentations of comparable material such as Joseph Howe's *Acadia* (written 1833–4) and William Kirby's *The U.E. – A Tale of Upper Canada* (1859). Goldsmith provides, almost by accident, a fascinating example of the problems of transplanting and adapting older literary models to newer requirements.

A discrepancy between content and language is even more evident in the work of Charles Sangster, who published *The St. Lawrence and the Saguenay* in 1856. The question posed by MacKay in *Quebec Hill* and quoted at the opening of this chapter becomes a perfect epigraph for any consideration of the title poem. Sangster was a native of Kingston, and he offers a poetic commentary on a voyage from Kingston down the St. Lawrence, past Montréal and Québec, and then up the Saguenay that was already famous for its wild beauty. His model is clearly Byron's *Childe Harold's Pilgrimage*, which Sangster follows not only in its basic pattern of Spenserian stanzas interspersed with short lyrics, and in its Romantic response to spectacular scenery, but in other suitably Byronic details. One of the Thousand Islands is even credited with a story about a 'stately Maiden' regularly crossing the river at 'wildest midnight' to visit her father, an outlawed 'Brigand Chief' (St. 9).

That the loyalty is to father rather than lover, however, marks the limits to Sangster's Byronism. Similarly, while the narrator is accompanied on his journey by a mysterious female form, at the end of the poem she is safely etherealized into a spirit of beauty. Above all, for Sangster the wilderness is automatically, or so it would seem, associated with God and religious certitude. On the voyage up the Saguenay, the ship takes him past scenes

> Whose unimaginable wildness fills
> The mind with joy insatiate, and weans
> The soul from earth, to Him whose Presence thrills
> All Beauty and all Truth.
>
> (St. 82)

Similarly, Cape Eternity (whose name is serendipitous for Sangster) looms up 'Like a God reigning in the Wilderness' (St. 95). There are numerous other instances – so frequent, indeed, as to become predictable; one begins to doubt whether Sangster would dare consider the possibility of a natural world outside divine control.

Here perhaps we encounter an intellectual and religious version of the linguistic problem confronting so many early Canadian poets. Sangster sees God in Nature because this is the connection he has been trained to make. Certainly his poetic vocabulary is inadequate to convey what he sees, let alone any subtle or original response to what he sees. Too often he displays a revealing insensitivity to words and meanings, and seems totally lacking in a sense of humour. Thus he can perpetrate lines like 'CAPE DIAMOND shows its sombre-coloured bust' (St. 49) and 'Keep the old Homestead sacred. What a night!' (St. 61). The poem retains an interest by reason of its subject matter but certainly not for the quality of its verse.

The rest of Sangster's poetry is similarly blemished. *Hesperus* appeared in 1860, and two manuscript collections, *Norland Echoes* and *The Angel Guest*, though never published in his lifetime, have since been made available. They contain little, however, that cannot be categorized as sententious uplift or embarrassing doggerel. Some of the 'Sonnets Written in the Orillia Woods' (in *Hesperus*) have a quiet introspective charm – and Sangster is here original enough to invent a variant on the strict form by ending each sonnet with an alexandrine – but they too are marred by prosaic thought and extraordinarily uneven diction. Like Charles Heavysege (see p. 170), he earnestly willed himself to be a poet but lacked the *sine qua non* of stylistic competence.

After the respectable pomposities of Sangster, it is a relief to turn to the down-to-earth, popular verse of Alexander McLachlan, whose 'Young Canada; or, Jack's as Good as his Master', with its celebration of 'The nobles of the forge and soil, / With ne'er a pedigree', gives a voice to the poorer nineteenth-century immigrants whose democratic enthusiasms so disturbed Moodie in the opening chapters of *Roughing It in the Bush*. McLachlan, who himself emigrated from Scotland in 1840, adopted Burns and the early Carlyle as his culture-heroes, and devoted his poetic energies to encouraging the downtrodden and oppressed to raise their own more equitable society in Canada which, they hoped, would prove the 'promised land of liberty' (*The Emigrant*, Ch. 2). His is the first notable example of what might be called proletarian verse in the country, and it contains a vigour and directness not achieved hitherto. Here was a new viewpoint and a new subject:

> We live in a rickety house,
> In a dirty dismal street,
> Where the naked hide from day,
> And thieves and drunkards meet.
>
> ('We Live in a Rickety House')

There is a passionate urgency about such verse that we have not met before.

But McLachlan's most significant contribution is undoubtedly his long poem *The Emigrant* (1861), in which the narrator, who describes himself as

> the very last
> Of that simple, hardy race
> Who first settled in this place,

presents a multifaceted version of the Ontario pioneering experience (Ch. 1). His unifying poetic voice is heard throughout the narrative, though it is interrupted by a series of poems in different verse forms assigned to different speakers. We hear from the narrator's 'grandsire' (Ch. 1), whose reported account takes us further back into history, 'Spouting Tom, nicknamed the preacher' (Ch. 2), 'old Aunty Jane' (Ch. 5), and several others. Thus the subject matter – establishing a new society in a new land, fear of the neighbouring Indians, etc. – recalls *The Rising Village*, while the intercalation of narrative, description, and song is closer to the form of *The St. Lawrence and the Saguenay* (though I know of no evidence that McLachlan was acquainted with either poem). In *The Emigrant* McLachlan has therefore succeeded in creating a form that allows him to intersperse his account with songs of sentimental nostalgia, rousing political verse, ballads, and love lyrics. From this poetic potpourri we receive a definite sense of community, of a motley collection of people in the process of building their own society.

The versification (especially the dominant octosyllabics) is often crude, and deliberately so. But it never settles into monotony; even the poetic gaucheries can be surprisingly effective. In the section entitled 'Cutting the First Tree' (Ch. 4), for example, the narrator confesses: 'We were awkward at the axe, / And the trees were stubborn facts.' At first we are tempted to attribute the lame rhyme to poetic negligence, yet there is a sense in which it can be justified. The refusal of the 'stubborn' alien trees to co-operate with the pre-established form is, in its own way, appropriate; or, from another perspective, the jarring off-rhyme can be said to embody the clumsiness of the workmen. The artificial polish of more sophisticated verse – the kind of effect that makes Moodie's genteel poems of pioneering so unsatisfying – would be totally out of place here. McLachlan is, I suspect, very much a hit-or-miss poet, and most of his other poems hold little interest for the modern reader. In *The Emigrant*, however, his subject is admirably suited to his strengths as a writer. Within the poem he describes the old traditional ballads as 'strains so void of art' that nevertheless contain 'the soul of poetry' and so 'live within the breast' (Ch. 5). The same could be said of his own poem. Moreover, it reminds us that rugged popular verse occurs early in the Canadian tradition, that the vernacular challenge to gentility has a long history. For all his obvious faults, McLachlan introduces a breath of badly needed fresh air into mid-Victorian Canadian literature.

Even more interesting, though decidedly controversial, is the work of Isabella Valancy Crawford, who published *Old Spookses' Pass, Malcolm's Katie, and Other Poems* at her own expense in 1884. A dialect poem set in the Rockies, 'Old Spookses' Pass' itself, with its vernacular presentation of an ordinary plain tale, suggests links with the verse of McLachlan, but whereas the latter was drawing upon his own experience and portraying the life and attitudes of his class, Crawford had to fall back upon her idiosyncratic but powerful imagination. The result, in her most characteristic work, is a poetry of colourful, inventive audacity. There is nothing quite like Crawford's poetry in nineteenth-century Canada, and it is not surprising that assessments of her writing vary radically. Thus for Clara Thomas she is, at her best, 'a true artist' (F. Tierney ed., *Isabella Valancy Crawford Symposium*, 1979, 126) while George Woodcock dismissed her as 'that truly awful poet' (*Taking It to the Letter*, 1981, 119). That Crawford possessed remarkable gifts is not to be doubted, but the development of her poetic talents was severely hampered by her literary seclusion (she lived in comparative isolation in Lakefield and Peterborough, and even in the final years of her life in Toronto made few contacts with writers or artists). Throughout her work there are flashes of an almost Blake-like imaginative intensity, but she did not possess the ultimate confidence in her powers that might have impelled her to follow an independent path. As a consequence, her occasionally dazzling imagistic clarity is surrounded with dull stretches of the tawdrily conventional. There are times when one wants to hail her as a Canadian Emily Brontë or Emily Dickinson; unfortunately, she can only be regarded as a Brontë or Dickinson *manqué*.

However, the handful of poems that prove to be gold rather than dross adds a new dimension to Canadian verse. They are remarkable not for any profundity of insight but for the consistency and clarity of their imagined world. 'Said the Canoe', for example, around which commentators have woven intricate symbolic and allegorical meanings, is best read straightforwardly as an impressively original poem in which an Indian encampment is seen, as the title indicates, from the viewpoint of a canoe. The boldness of the imagery is conspicuous:

> The darkness built its wigwam walls
>> Close round the camp, and at its curtain
>> Pressed shapes, thin, woven and uncertain
> As white locks of tall waterfalls.

Here and in poems such as 'The Camp of Souls' and 'The Lily-Bed', Crawford is the first significant poet within the English-Canadian tradition to recognize the rich treasure of image and reference to be found in the life and culture of the Indian peoples. At her best, however, she can go beyond these to create her own distinctive versions of universal myths. In 'The Dark Stag' the simple process of night yielding to day is transformed into a cosmic battle between hunted stag and hunter sun:

> A startled stag, the blue-grey Night,
>> Leaps down beyond black pines.
> Behind – a length of yellow light –
>> The hunter's arrow shines.
> His moccasins are stained with red,
>> He bends upon his knee,
> From covering peaks his shafts are sped,
> The blue mists plume his mighty head, –
>> Well may the swift Night flee!

Often, indeed, with their strong sense of colour and boldly archetypal situations, her poems take on the qualities of primitive art.

Crawford is best known for her long poem 'Malcolm's Katie', though its pre-eminence is not, I think, fully justified. The conventional nineteenth-century story involves Katie, only daughter of a mildly possessive widowed father, her love for Max, and the attempts of a false friend Adrian to deceive her. It begins charmingly if predictably with a vow of loyalty between lover and beloved, soon gets bogged down in demonic deceptions, falling timber, and accidents in log-jams, and ultimately collapses in melodramatic death leaps and rescues at the psychological moment. Some commentators have tried to play down the absurdities of the plot on a realistic level by emphasizing symbolic meanings. James Reaney, who sees Crawford as a profoundly mythopoeic poet, maintained in an early article that, since she was constructing 'a myth about the whole business of being a Canadian she has no time to fret about making the poem vulgarly believable in the low mimetic [i.e., realistic] areas' (R. McDougall, ed., *Our Living Tradition*, 2nd and 3rd Series, 1959, 284). But the histrionic posturings can hardly be dismissed so easily. Reaney is right to draw our attention to the most characteristic and successful parts of the poem, wrong to pretend that the formal incoherence of the whole is unimportant.

As before, Crawford distinguishes herself in background description which displays an obstinate insistence on moving into the foreground. The narrative is punctuated by a series of set pieces relating to the passing of the seasons, and Crawford gains a special effect by presenting her conventional love triangle against the exotic imagery of the Indian land. Here, for example, is the coming of winter:

> From the far wigwam sprang the strong North Wind
> And rushed with war-cry down the steep ravines,
> And wrestled with the giants of the woods ...
> And smote his whistling arrows o'er the plains.
>
> (Part 4)

Moreover, a single simile can transform a commonplace observation into an imaginative event: 'The crackling ice-beds scolded harsh like squaws' (Part 2). E. K. Brown claimed that Crawford's 'fantastic imagination' (*On Canadian Poetry* 43) was a weakness as well as a strength, and it is certainly true that, when her inspiration flags, the descent from peak to abyss is all the more conspicuous. She never quite solved the relation between her primitivistic visual imagination and her narrative form. Her reach may well have exceeded her grasp, but she nevertheless left the vision of a vision.

The poets I have so far discussed worked in isolation. They rarely enjoyed the company, criticism, and encouragement of their fellow practitioners. The so-called Confederation Poets – Charles G. D. Roberts, Bliss Carman, Archibald Lampman, and Duncan Campbell Scott – are poorly named since none was more than seven years old at the time of Canadian Confederation in 1867. The phrase has an unintentional aptness, however; although they were in no sense a tightly knit group, they unwittingly formed a loose confederation among themselves. Through personal friendships, meetings, correspondence, and the regular reading of each other's work, they came to be associated together in their own minds, and later in the minds of the literary public. They were seen not as four poets writing in Canada but as the most distinguished representatives of a generation of Canadian poets. Above all, though influenced by both British and American models, they gradually evolved styles and attitudes that could be recognized, at home and abroad, as characteristic of the new Dominion.

Roberts was the most energetic and precocious of the group, publishing his first volume, *Orion and Other Poems* (1880), which proved a considerable inspiration to the rest, at the early age of twenty. Here the English poetic tradition is evident; the book is full of echoes of, among others, Wordsworth, Keats, Tennyson, and Swinburne. In a last-minute 'Dedication' included at the end of the book, he describes the contents accurately enough as concerned with 'alien matters in distant regions', but Roberts used these imported materials to sharpen his technique and gain experience in a wide range of stanza patterns and poetic forms. This apprenticeship bore fruit in his next volume, *In Divers Tones* (1886), which contains some of the poems by which he is best remembered.

Of these 'Tantramar Revisited' is perhaps the most remarkable. Significantly, Roberts here chooses a subject close to home, the Tantramar Marshes on the border of New Brunswick and Nova Scotia which he had known intimately as a boy. Although the verse form, a variant of the classical hexameter, may recall the example of earlier poets – Clough, Swinburne, Longfellow, Lanier – Roberts here adapts it to his own purposes and renders it subservient to the rhythms of his own poetic voice. The theme is conventional enough: the poet-narrator returns to his home-land, looks down upon it from a hill, and meditates on past and present. But the specific details are finely etched, and Roberts establishes a tone that tempers a sympathetic nostalgia with a strong sense of personal immediacy:

> Yet, as I sit and watch, the present peace of the landscape, –
> Stranded boats, those reels empty and idle, the hush,
> One grey hawk slow-wheeling above yon cluster of haystacks, –
> More than the old-time stir this stillness welcomes me home.

There is nothing perfunctory about this sentiment; we hear the controlled rhythms of an individual poet.

There are also a number of impressive sonnets in this collection, several of which appear in a more appropriate context in his next full-length volume, *Songs of the Common Day* (1893). Here Roberts takes the traditional sonnet form but, instead of concentrating on unity of thought, uses it for a series of descriptive miniatures portraying life and nature in the Maritimes. Aiming to make 'dull, familiar things divine' ('Prologue'), he draws upon all his verbal resources to create scenes that are both exact and evocative, displaying in particular a wide range of sensual impressions. In 'The Mowing', for instance, the emphasis is on sound:

> This is the voice of high midsummer's heat,
> The rasping vibrant clamour soars and shrills
> O'er all the meadowy range of shadeless hills,
> As if a host of giant cicadae beat
> The cymbals of their wings with tireless feet ...

This may not be unquestionably great poetry, but it is both confident and competent, and it begins the much-needed task of expressing Canada and its landscape in poetic terms. In establishing his own voice within a traditional poetic structure, Roberts attains a characteristic and significant balance between the sanctioned methods of the Old World and the fresh approaches of the New.

He never succeeded, however, in going beyond the extraordinary promise of his early verse. On leaving Canada for the United States and Europe in 1897, Roberts encountered a host of new influences, but was shackled by his restless nature and technical facility. His subsequent poetry is generally eloquent and smooth-flowing – he had an enviable gift for the evocative lyric – but a corresponding depth failed to materialize. He felt the need to write inspiring, elevating verse, which he brought together in the 1936 *Selected Poems* under the heading of 'Poems Philosophical and Mystical', but he had a weakness for the pseudo-profound and was liable to be betrayed into vague, awesome statements professing a higher seriousness which they never quite achieve. Until his return to Canada in 1925, his best work is to be found in his animal stories, but he enjoyed a poetic flowering towards the end of his life when, though still conforming to the obsolescent poetic assumptions of the late nineteenth century, he nevertheless regained much of his earlier effectiveness. 'The Iceberg', a long poem written in the early 1930s, is of special interest because, following the pattern of his animal chronicles, it traces the course of an iceberg from its spawning 'A thousand miles due north / Beyond Cape Chidley' to the moment when it 'merged forever in the all-solvent sea' of warmer latitudes. Roberts has boldly employed a first-person narrative voice here so that the poem expresses the action of a natural force harshly independent of humanity. The poem appeared contemporaneously with the early work of E. J. Pratt (Roberts had written an introduction to Pratt's *Verses by the Sea* in 1930), and provides one example among several of the verbal and thematic continuity between the two poets.

Bliss Carman was Roberts's cousin. The two had known each other since childhood and both attended the University of New Brunswick (a verse 'Epistle to Bliss Carman', written at the time, appears in *Orion*). They shared, too, a poetic restlessness; words like 'wandering' and 'vagrancy' recur in their verse. But Carman took over more completely than Roberts the myth of the poet as romantic dreamer and unfettered Bohemian. In their own generation he enjoyed the wider following, but time has been decidedly less kind to his reputation. Carman resembled Roberts in being a lover of the classics and an enthusiast for inspiring and high-sounding verse, but he possessed a narrower range and a less sure poetic technique. The name poem in his first volume, 'Low Tide on

Grand Pré', remains his most satisfying poem with its hauntingly elusive sense of loss and unspecified melancholy:

> Was it a year or lives ago
> We took the grasses in our hands,
> And caught the summer flying low
> Over the waving meadow lands
> And held it there between our hands?

A personal urgency is communicated here, though Carman's biographers are uncertain whether the poem laments the death of a beloved girl or of his mother. This doubt perhaps offers a clue to the poem's success. The emotion is firmly communicated, but the object of the emotion remains vague, with the result that readers are free to adapt it to their own situations. The language is crisp and controlled ('*caught* the summer flying low'), the rhythms subtle, and these are qualities for which Carman cannot often be praised. Above all, the poem is concise and economical, unlike so much of his verse that has an unfortunate tendency to ramble.

Carman was widely read in his own time because he produced poems that conformed to popular preconceptions about what poetry ought to be. He wrote of love and loss; his imagery was drawn from conventionally poetic subjects – flowers, sunsets, the sea, the seasons (especially autumn) – with frequent reference to dreams and enchantment. His rhythms were conspicuous (often, indeed, rollicking), and his verse was strewn with bright and emphatic colours: one of his better poems, 'The Eavesdropper', refers to 'earth-brown eyes', the 'blue dusk' of a beloved's hair, 'a yellow maple tree', 'the purple twilight,' hills that are 'sinister and black'. Above all, his collaboration with the American poet Richard Hovey in *Songs from Vagabondia* (1894) and subsequent volumes, which briskly sang of the 'joys of the open road', gave him a reputation for daring Bohemianism that was in fact unjustified.

At his best, he could achieve a resonant eloquence. Here is the opening stanza of a poem with the suitably pretentious title, 'At the Great Release':

> When the black horses from the house of Dis
> Stop at my door and the dread charioteer

Knocks at my portal, summoning me to go
On the far solitary unknown way
Where all the race of men fare and are lost,
Fleeting and numerous as the autumnal leaves
Before the wind in Lesbos of the Isles …

For modern sophisticated taste, this relies excessively on stock responses to the mystery of death, on a combination of dreamy spirituality and awesome vagueness that studiously avoids the challenge of hard thought. At the same time, it is memorable (even unforgettable) and its tone – whatever we may ultimately think of its quality – is admirably sustained. Characteristically, Carman takes classical references and clothes them in a romantic melancholy. One of his volumes that can still be read with considerable pleasure is *Sappho* (1904), which contained an appreciative introduction by Roberts. Here Carman attempts to reconstruct the lost lyrics of the Greek poetess and then proceeds to 'translate' them into English verse. The result would be unlikely to impress a classical scholar, but that is hardly the point. Carman is engaged not so much in translation in the conventional sense as in imitation and transmutation. Sappho is herself, as it were, translated from the sixth century BC to the ethos of the *fin-de-siècle* 1890s. She is imagined as expressing herself as if she belonged to the modern period while maintaining the Mediterranean clarity of her own time and place. Sometimes the verse is richly eloquent as in the following (based, as it happens, on one of the few surviving Sappho fragments):

I loved thee, Atthis, in the long ago
When the great oleanders were in flower
In the broad herded meadows full of sun.

(No. 23)

More often, Carman achieves a piercing simplicity that once again is all the more effective for its being easily transferable to the circumstances of the reader's personal experience:

Softer than the hill-fog to the forest
Are the loving hands of my dear lover,

When she sleeps beside me in the starlight
And her beauty drenches me with rest.

(No. 45)

Carman wrote voluminously and had little power of self-criticism. Out of his many volumes a handful of romantic and generally sad lyrical poems attains an exquisite sensuousness. His was a decidedly minor talent, but his best poems exhibit a frail yet palpable resilience.

Archibald Lampman also came to be seen as embodying the classic pattern of a poet's life, though for rather different reasons. A sensitive man forced into uncongenial clerical work and a city life that he found oppressive, he escaped into the country at every opportunity and wrote richly textured verse that combined generally rural description with an inspiring and acceptable moral message. His early death at the age of thirty-eight, the neglect of his poetry during his lifetime, and subsequent revelations about a frustrating love affair have all helped to establish the archetypal form of a poetic career. 'The Canadian Keats' became a convenient label, doubly unfortunate because (as Lampman himself well knew) he was not in Keats's class but, more crucially, because the phrase presents an earnestly Canadian poet in an inappropriate setting and obscures the limited but genuine originality that he assuredly possessed.

Many of Lampman's poems take their titles from seasons or rural places and offer minute descriptions (generally from the Ottawa Valley) that are more detailed though less varied than those of Roberts. They also display an admirable emotional restraint. Thus 'In October' begins:

Along the waste, a great way off, the pines
    Like tall slim priests of storm, stand up and bar
The low long strip of dolorous red that lines
    The under west, where wet winds moan afar.
The cornfields all are brown, and brown the meadows
    With the blown leaves' wind-heapèd traceries,
And the brown thistle stems that cast no shadows,
    And bear no bloom for bees.

'Wind-heapèd traceries' explains the 'Canadian Keats' tag, but the rest of the stanza, with its curiously complex image of 'priests of storm' and a painterly emphasis on the browns of autumn, offers an unequivocally Canadian scene and is representative of the capacity of the Confederation Poets in general to create modestly distinctive verse without breaking away too conspicuously from the established traditions of literature in English. What Lampman failed to learn from the English Romantics, however, was the need to vary both tone and viewpoint. His descriptive poems can continue like this for stanza after stanza until the effect is cloying. Too many of his poems reiterate the same basic pattern: the poet is renewed within natural scenery, is offered an opportunity for uninterrupted meditation, and can return to the city refreshed. Lampman frequently tells us how his experiences provoke thought but less often communicates that thought. In discipline and texture his poetry outshines Carman's and all but the best of Roberts's, but it does not always escape the lapse into tonal monotony.

Like the other Confederation Poets, Lampman tended to overemphasize imagery of dream and reverie, produced reams of poetic uplift in the moralistic Victorian style that soon alienates modern readers, and was at his best when he concentrated on the poetic medium and left the prosaic message to look after itself. Most of his best poems, through the good offices of anthologists, have been separated from the mass of his work, and are now well known. Among these are a number of sonnets, a form which Lampman, like Roberts, found especially congenial, and for similar reasons. They include 'Winter Evening', with its vigorously auspicious opening, 'To-night the very horses springing by / Toss gold from whitened nostrils', and 'A Dawn on the Lièvre', with its powerful telescoping of natural, but in this context magical, Canadian images:

> Full on the shrouded night-charged river broke
> The sun, down the long mountain valley rolled,
> A sudden swinging avalanche of gold,
> Through mists that sprang and reeled aside like smoke.

But Lampman could handle other forms with similar skill, and is often particularly effective with octosyllabics. Few have re-created the languid oppressiveness of high summer more successfully than Lampman in these often quoted lines from 'Heat':

From plains that reel to southward, dim,
   The road runs by me white and bare;
Up the steep hill it seems to swim
   Beyond, and melt into the glare.
Upward half-way, or it may be
   Nearer the summit, slowly steals
A hay-cart, moving dustily
   With idly clacking wheels.

'The City at the End of Things', though somewhat too shrilly melodramatic for some tastes, achieves a striking awesomeness in imagining a world of deadened mechanism, a nightmare vision that recurs in Canadian literature, notably in Grove's *The Master of the Mill*. For Lampman it becomes an emblem of demonic apocalypse:

The roar shall vanish at its height,
And over that tremendous town
The silence of eternal night
Shall gather close and settle down.
All its grim grandeur, tower and hall,
Shall be abandoned utterly,
And into rust and dust shall fall
From century to century.

More effective, because both more varied and more restrained, is 'In November', in which a Wordsworthian spot of time is fully acclimatized to a Canadian environment. One wintry day Lampman comes upon a clearing in the woods 'peopled' (his own word) by scores of dead mullein stalks; startled by the experience, he finds himself thinking of them not as plants but as

     some spare company
Of hermit folk, who long ago,
Wandering in bodies to and fro,
Had chanced upon this lonely way,

And rested thus, till death one day
Surprised them at their compline prayer
And left them standing lifeless there.

Later, the wintry sunlight conveys upon the scene 'A sort of spectral happiness', and the poem is admirably balanced between affirmation and melancholy. For once Lampman dramatizes his own situation, distances it, and so transcends it. The exquisitely poised epithets (the poem ends with the communication of 'A pleasure secret and austere') contribute to a minor classic within the Canadian tradition and catch the engaging sharpness of the Canadian landscape that will later impress poets like A. J. M. Smith and F. R. Scott.

A number of Lampman's most effective poems – 'Morning on the Lièvre', for instance, as well as the sonnet, 'A Dawn on the Lièvre', already mentioned – are the product of canoe trips into the northern bush, and on several of these Duncan Campbell Scott was his companion. Even more than Lampman, Scott responded to the remote landscapes of wilderness, forest, water, and rock. A civil servant who spent most of his life in the Department of Indian Affairs, he made several formal tours of inspection into the wilds to meet with Indian tribes, and out of these expeditions came the most conspicuously successful of his poems. It seems as if Scott deflected into his poetry the emotional sympathies he was unable to display as an official. His main subject is the fatal but inevitable meeting-point of Indian and white. This is memorably evoked in 'Night Hymns on Lake Nipigon', where

on the lonely, loon-haunted Nipigon reaches
Rises the hymn of triumph and courage and comfort,
'Adeste fideles'.

In the world of his Indian poems there is much courage (in 'The Forsaken', for example) but neither triumph nor comfort. The Indian mother in the sonnet 'The Onondaga Madonna' (where the juxtaposition of cultures is strikingly evident in the title) belongs to a 'waning race', while her child is not a saviour but 'The latest promise of her nation's doom'. Elsewhere, an Indian trapper is murdered by white men, 'servants of greed', for the furs he is apparently carrying on his toboggan; in fact, he is taking the body of his dead wife for burial, and the title, 'On the Way to the Mission', signals the bitter irony. And in the most haunting of his poems, 'Powassan's Drum', the world of the white man listens with combined horror and fascination 'To the throb–throb–throb–throb– / Throbbing of Powassan's drum'.

Part of the effectiveness of Scott's Indian poems lies in their avoidance of easy solutions. In general, the poetry of Lampman and Scott differs from that of Carman and even much of Roberts in that it is less direct and assertive. Scott is particularly fond of emphasizing narrative forms in which his themes can be dramatized, not just proclaimed as poetic wisdom. His poetry appeals to contemporary readers, indeed, because it is written out of his doubts rather than his certainties. He admires much of Indian life, and deplores much, and he is convinced that nothing can reverse the pattern of decline. But the Indian is also seen as an image of mankind, and so becomes a medium for Scott's persuasive and stoic pessimism. 'The Height of Land' is perhaps his most central poem. Located on the watershed between 'The lonely north enlaced with lakes and streams' and 'The crowded southern land / With all the welter of the lives of men' – that is, between the worlds of Indian and white – it takes the form of a meditation by the insomniac Scott while his Indian guides are 'dead asleep'. Scott is here at his most Arnoldian, and he broods uneasily upon the polarities of life – on the spiritual and the material, on beauty and terror, on hope for the future always tempered with a sober awareness of the complexities of the present. An intensely didactic poem, it is saved by the sincere tentativeness of Scott's questionings, by the controlled but uncertain rhythms in which they are expressed, and above all by its total organization: the intellectual within the wilderness that troubles him contrasted with the Indians who lack the divine curse of poetic introspection.

Scott's poetry is not always about Indians, however. 'The Piper of Arll' (which reversed the usual direction of transatlantic influence since it inspired John Masefield to become a poet) is a lyrical, richly mysterious narrative poem not unlike some of Carman's though better sustained. But 'Chiostro Verde', from *The Green Cloister* (1935), describing a visit to Santa Maria Novella in Florence, is more typical of Scott's rhythmical and imagistic spareness:

Under the roof of the cloister
A few frescoes are clinging
Made by Paolo Uccello,
Once they were clear and mellow,
Now they have fallen away
To a dull green-grey,
What has not fallen will fall.

We notice here Scott's characteristic blending of a Victorian traditionalism (he is close to the cadences of Arnold's 'Rugby Chapel') with a
modern avoidance of the verbally ornate and an equally modern concern
(though again via Arnold) for honest precision, 'seeing the object as it
really is'. Scott's musical interests led him to make far subtler variations on
metrical norms than the other Confederation Poets, and although this
sometimes results in a kind of rhythmical stutter, it more often enables
him to achieve technical effects from which later poets have learned. Less
admired in his time, Scott is now recognized among the Confederation
group as the one who established the most effective lines of poetic continuity between nineteenth- and twentieth-century Canadian verse.

Chapter 3

The Beginnings in Fiction

The Canadian fictional tradition began late. While a considerable number of novels and short stories appeared in the course of the nineteenth century, their quality is in the main disappointing, and the prime reasons for this are by no means difficult to discover. Fiction depends upon a developed and preferably closely knit society; it generally concerns itself with customs and manners, with obedience to or rebellion against established communal norms. The historical situation in early Canada may well have fostered tall tales and popular stories of adventure, but it hardly encouraged the sophisticated analysis of human motives, attitudes, and relationships. More practical considerations also proved discouraging. In economic terms, fiction requires the nucleus of a thoughtful and loyal reading public that simply did not exist in Canada at that time. Canadian novelists could not expect to gain a hearing unless they found an audience – and, perhaps even more important, their principal publisher – outside Canada. So far as serious fiction was concerned, Canadian readers relied for the most part upon cheap reprints of British and American works. Markets for short stories or the serializing of novels were to all intents and purposes confined to British and American outlets. Above all, the time when Canadian fiction might have begun to develop coincided with the great flowering of the English novel in the age dominated by Dickens, George Eliot, and Thackeray.

Small wonder, then, that a native fiction failed to materialize in any noticeable form until well into the twentieth century. What we have, until after the First World War, is a series of isolated fictions, interestingly representative of their particular kinds, but following various conventions and seldom bearing much resemblance to each other. They are, for the most part, individual experiments – pioneering efforts that may well be historically significant but only rarely, or fitfully, attain an unquestionable artistic standard. They are often derivative, but far less often successfully acclimatized. In the pages that follow, then, I shall be considering individual works rather than individual authors, and will attempt to show their significance as representative types.

Frances Brooke's *The History of Emily Montague*, published as early as 1769, has been claimed not only as the first Canadian but even as the first North American novel. A literary inhabitant of the Augustan world of Dr Johnson, David Garrick, and Fanny Burney, Brooke spent some five years in Québec in the mid-1760s while her husband was chaplain to the English garrison. *The History of Emily Montague* is an epistolary novel in the manner of Richardson's *Clarissa*. It begins with the arrival of the hero, Colonel Rivers, to take up land in Canada, much of the central action taking place in the immediate environs of Québec, and ends when most of the characters have returned to England. The unremarkable plot recounts the inevitable obstacles that arise before all the leading participants are suitably paired off, and exists, like so many minor eighteenth-century equivalents, as a convenient peg upon which to hang generalizations about morality, religion, love, the conventions of courtship – and, in this case, a detailed account of the social life of an English military garrison in the years immediately after the fall of New France.

If, therefore, we still read *The History of Emily Montague*, it is not so much for its novelistic as for its non-fiction, documentary qualities. Brooke gives us a fascinating glimpse of the Québec garrison that, because no longer active in a military capacity, is in the process of forming itself into an identifiable society. It is, of course, little more than a reproduction of English mores and customs, but excursions to the Montmorency Falls and the Kamouraska region, and accounts of the necessary adaptations to extreme climatic conditions add touches of unique local colour. We see Brooke (like Traill and Moodie and so many others in the century after her) struggling with the difficulty of employing standard artistic terminology in order to describe a new landscape, and discovering in Canadian scenery the Burkean *'great sublime'* as well as the merely *'beautiful'* (Letter 2). She even goes to the extreme of inserting a series of letters from William Fermor to a mysterious Earl of ——, irrelevant to the main plot, offering a comprehensive account of 'the political and religious state of Canada' which claims to be based on 'the best information available' (Letter 87).

But the crucial point to be made about the book is that it was published in England and addressed to an English audience for whom, in the decade after Wolfe's defeat of Montcalm, Canada was at least temporarily a fashionable and even exotic locale. One of his English friends offers an imaginative picture of the hero 'chasing females wild as the wind thro' woods as wild as themselves' (Letter 3), and much of the novel attempts, in almost tourist-guide style, to present a more accurate and informative account. Brooke is a clear, accomplished, often witty, but not particularly original writer, and her single 'Canadian' work is best described as an English novel that happens to exploit Canadian subject matter. It is essentially an outsider's view, but no less valuable for that. Its author is, however, Canada's first but by no means last literary bird of passage. Within the Canadian tradition her book represents an interesting beginning but also a dead end.

With John Richardson's *Wacousta* (1832) we move into the realm of historical romance. Though the action is virtually contemporaneous with that of *The History of Emily Montague,* the book was written seventy years after the period in question, and Richardson employs a different set of literary conventions to portray a totally different world. He focuses upon Pontiac's attacks on the British forts in the Great Lakes area in 1763, and presents detailed and lurid accounts of the fall of Michilimackinac (where Alexander Henry had been among the few to escape) and the foiled attempt on Fort Detroit. These events are important in the history of British North America, and the white/Indian antagonisms have consequences for the later history of Canada and for the future relations of white Canadians with the native peoples. It is perhaps because of the undoubted thematic importance of the material that *Wacousta* has been so grotesquely overrated within the Canadian fictional tradition.

Richardson could hardly have attempted historical fiction in the early 1830s without feeling himself under the shadow of Sir Walter Scott, and the origins of the personal (as distinct from the national) feud that dominates the novel go back appropriately to the Scottish Highlands. The heroine's grandfather had been a rebel in the Jacobite rebellion of 1715, and was living in hermit-like seclusion with his daughter. Colonel de Haldimar, commander at Fort Detroit, had while an ensign stolen the girl's affections from his friend Reginald Morton, who brings about his elaborate revenge by disguising himself as an Indian and organizing Pontiac's forces under the name of Wacousta. It is Wacousta who blends the personal feud into the national one (to seek revenge he joins the Scots in the 1745 rebellion and then offers his services to Montcalm at Québec), and this seems to me the fatal flaw in the book. There is a gap between private and public actions and motives that does not occur in the best of Scott. Moreover, a subtly critical intelligence is discernible behind Scott's most romantic conventions, and its equivalent is distressingly absent in Richardson.

If one is not troubled by excessive coincidence, inconsistency of character, and all the stock devices of Gothic horror, the story is exciting on a very basic level. Richardson can certainly create and maintain suspense, and many of the scenes, especially those involving nocturnal escapades and terrors, are decidedly effective. But for the serious reader the interest quickly palls. As horror piles upon horror, the unrelieved tone of excitement soon becomes oppressive. Virtually every chapter is punctuated by shrieks, scalps are continually reeking, and in his scenes of conflict Richardson apparently works on the principle: the more blood the better. The factitious quality of the whole conception is particularly disturbing. De Haldimar's seduction of Wacousta's bride-to-be is inexplicable in view of the rest of his character (not to mention hers), and it cannot carry the burden of Wacousta's subsequent psychopathic vengeance. It is, however, Richardson's style that most clearly betrays the tawdriness of his novelistic powers. He writes a clotted, prolix, graceless prose, and his dialogue is particularly stilted ("'Ha, ha, ha!' laughed the savage in a low triumphant tone, "the place of our meeting is well timed, though somewhat singular, it must be confessed"', Book II, Ch. 2). Sometimes it is difficult not to suspect parody: in one scene, one of de Haldimar's sons is almost recaptured by hostile Indians because, while in hiding, he kisses a friendly Indian so passionately that she falls off a log. Absurdities abound, and the writing rarely tempts us to forgive the lack of credibility. Here and in *Wacousta*'s sequel, *The Canadian Brothers* (1840), which extends the feud up to the War of 1812 (in which Richardson served as a boy), the novelist leaves no cliché unturned. He employs some powerful and psychologically significant themes, but never raises them above the level of soap opera or Hollywood B film. His, indeed, is the classic example of the inability of fiction to attain literary excellence in the absence of intellectual depth and stylistic expertise.

William Kirby's *The Golden Dog* (1877), another historical romance but bearing little resemblance to *Wacousta*, is set in the years immediately preceding the fall of New France in 1759. Kirby, a Tory Loyalist and indifferent poet, had prefaced his long poem *The U. E.* (1859) by stating that 'its design was mainly to preserve a few peculiar traits of a generation of men, now alas! nearly passed away', and *The Golden Dog* similarly looks back to the ideals of a vanished society. It is a world of intrigue and violence in which the chivalric values of the old regime and the *honnêtes gens* are being replaced by the cut-throat rivalries of the new commerce. Most of the main characters are historical, but the stories on which the fiction is based belong rather to legend than to authentic history. More romance than novel, *The Golden Dog* inherits the binary conventions of romance – the fidelity and piety of Amélie de Repentigny against the sexual opportunism and intrigue of Angélique des Meloises, the honest trading of Bourgeois Philibert against blatant exploitation by the Grand Company and Intendant Bigot. It is a world of heroes and villains, of right against wrong, of the idealized old against the cynical and corrupt new.

It has often been claimed that Kirby merely repeated the romantic formulae evolved by Scott and the elder Dumas, but this is not altogether fair. His work, though diligently researched, lacks the historical foundation of the best of the Waverley Novels, and the leisurely pace and repetitive style, though not unrelated to the practice of his predecessors, results in a very different effect. A curious tension is produced between the exaggerated emotions and romantic actions on the one hand, and the lovingly minute and factually exact descriptions of houses, public buildings, feasts, and local customs on the other. The plot is continually interrupted, and the suspense thereby increased, by extended genre pictures that superficially read like digressions but frequently prove the most memorable parts of the book. All is seen as if through a gauze of romance, and even the more absurd manipulations of plot and simplistic motivations (often reminiscent of opera scenarios) take on a singular charm. The events in the story are filtered through Kirby's stiff but consistently dignified prose, and even when the willing suspension of disbelief is hardest, narrative interest is maintained. The principal characters may seem too good (or too bad) to be true, but they nevertheless achieve a human individuality. For all its faults (especially conspicuous if we persist in evoking the hardly relevant criteria of realistic fiction), this is perhaps the most substantial narrative written in Canada in the nineteenth century.

Although not published until after the author's death, James De Mille's *A Strange Manuscript Found in a Copper Cylinder* (1888) may well date back as far as the late 1860s. It is a combination of fantasy and social satire. Four Englishmen (a lord, a writer, a doctor, and an academic linguist), becalmed on a yacht near the Canaries, retrieve from the sea a manuscript account by an Adam More (both names are significant) who has discovered an unknown Antarctic land. They read out sections of the manuscript in turn, and discuss it according to their particular interests and expertise. The presentation of More's adventures is relatively feeble as a plot, but his portrayal of the Kosekin, the strange inhabitants of this land, is absorbing. They partake in a form of cannibalism (a reductive parody of the Catholic Mass?), prefer darkness to light (a comment on human fallibility?), worship poverty and long for death (allusions to Victorian society in which commercial materialism existed side by side with pious beliefs about love of money as the root of all evil and the existence of a better world beyond the grave?). Like Thomas More in *Utopia*, Swift in *Gulliver's Travels*, and Samuel Butler in *Erewhon* (which may or may not have appeared after he began work on the book), De Mille can use his imagined land to comment generally on human behaviour and to satirize particular aspects of his own society. He is at his best when the more unlikely principles of the Kosekin are found to have disturbing connections with contemporary life. For example, the Kohen, priest-leader of the Kosekin, remarks to Adam: 'You, with your pretended fear of death, wish to meet it in battle as eagerly as we do, and your most renowned men are those who have sent most to death' (Ch. 18).

A Strange Manuscript is in some respects the most intelligent and most probing piece of fictional writing in nineteenth-century Canada, and the potential sophistication of its frame-device is of considerable interest. Unfortunately, the book is clearly unfinished. The closing account, in which More and his Kosekin beloved are triumphant over those who attempt to sacrifice them, fails to connect with the context of danger in which the manuscript purports to be written. And the final paragraph reads as a perfunctory ending that blatantly breaks off what has not been formally concluded. More radically, there exists an uneasy tonal discrepancy between the often absurd details of the adventure story (a chase on tame pterodactyls, for instance) and the mature cogency of the book's satirical implications. It seems to have been written deliberately for the British market – all the characters except the Kosekin themselves are English – and it belongs to a tradition of socio-political fantasy that has never flourished in Canada. It is perhaps important, apart from its intrinsic merits, as an example of the kind of talent that might have developed at this period if a discriminating readership and literary tradition had existed in the country at that time. De Mille's other writings are for the most part pitched at a popular level, and this one foray into fiction of more permanent interest proved singularly abortive.

Some of the best fictional writing in the twentieth century has employed the short-story form, and here again the nineteenth-century examples seem little more than pale shadows of the later achievement. The more popular collections of the period, like Gilbert Parker's *Pierre and His People* (1892) and E. W. Thomson's *Old Man Savarin* (1895), relied for the most part on thrilling or sentimental plots and homely characterization, and now seem stereotyped and obvious to modern readers. Although sharing these qualities, one collection escapes their limitations through its stylistic and technical expertise. This is Duncan Campbell Scott's *In the Village of Viger* (1896). Scott offers the stories in Arcadian or pastoral terms, but in fact they vary radically in tone from the tender and idyllic to the Gothic and sombre. All are unified by their setting in a rural French-Canadian village portrayed with humour but without condescension, and by the quiet but firm control of Scott's narration. Each story is absorbing in itself, but together they build up a convincing sense of a particular communal life with recurring characters, a consistent background, and an emotional atmosphere that alters with the mood of each story but remains stable in terms of the whole book. Scott devoted most of his creative energies to poetry, and in later years only fitfully exercised his talents for short fiction, but his contribution was important historically because it demonstrated the virtues of care and finish in a form that hitherto had rarely been approached with artistic seriousness.*

At about the same time the short-story form was developed for very different purposes by Ernest Thompson Seton and Scott's fellow poet

---

* For a shrewd challenge to this judgment, see John Metcalf's *What Is a Canadian Literature?* (45–87, especially 77–79).

Charles G. D. Roberts. They were the first to realize that the animal world of forest and wilderness was an area virtually uncharted and unchronicled in literature. The realistic animal story (as distinct from the age-old beast fable) is in fact the one genre that can confidently be claimed as a native Canadian art form, and it is of course appropriate that such a genre should develop in a country where unsettled and uninhabitable land still predominated. Seton and Roberts were exact contemporaries, and it is difficult to assign to one rather than the other the credit for inventing the form. Roberts published his first book of animal stories, *Earth's Enigmas,* in 1896, two years before Seton's *Wild Animals I Have Known.* Seton, however, had published 'The Prairie Chicken' as early as 1883. This is a factual scientific article, but Seton, though more of a professional naturalist than Roberts, was always tempted to develop his observations into continuous narratives. In many of his best stories, like 'Lobo, King of the Currumpaw', 'Silver-spot: The Story of a Crow' (both in his first collection) and 'The Winnipeg Wolf' (in *Animal Heroes,* 1905), Seton is himself either participant or observer. Other stories, like 'Krag, the Kootenay Ram' (in *Lives of the Hunted,* 1901), are expanded from accounts he had heard from hunters and trappers. As often as not these stories take the form of fictional animal biographies. 'The material of the accounts is true', he wrote in the prefatory note to *Lives of the Hunted.* 'The chief liberty taken is in ascribing to one animal the adventures of several.' Seton's stories usually exist in a no man's land between fiction and non-fiction; his fiction invariably has a non-fiction purpose in that it is representative, illustrative of events continually taking place in the wilderness.

Much the same might be said of Roberts. Nevertheless, although some of his most successful stories, like 'The King of the Mamozekel', the story of a moose (in *The Kindred of the Wild,* 1902), follow Seton's pattern of the animal biography, Roberts approached the animal world more deliberately as a writer of fiction. He is more conscious of the animals at the centres of his stories as part of the totality of the natural world, and therefore evokes a more memorable impression of the wild. His focus is as much on 'the ancient wood', 'the wilderness', 'the silences', as on the animal protagonists. Both writers present a Darwinian universe in which the survival of the fittest prevails as a basic law of nature. In consequence, both like to portray individuals of the species who, because of their extra strength or cunning, are superior to the rest of their kind. But Roberts is insistent on pointing up the extent to which humanity belongs to this world. For him, human beings and animals are equally 'kindred of the wild'. In his first animal story, 'Do Seek Their Meat from God' (which opens *Earth's Enigmas*), two panthers attempt to kill a human child in order to feed their own young. This tale represents a variant on numerous subsequent stories in which the offspring of one animal or bird dies so that the offspring of another may live. Roberts rarely draws attention to the hard truth behind his narratives, but they convey a quite profound insight into the natural world and the basic conditions of life that pertain as much to ourselves as to the 'wild kindred'.

Both writers were accused of investing their animal protagonists with human attributes, and in this respect, because he was more ambitious as a writer, Roberts took greater risks than Seton. On the other hand, though he may at times have anthropomorphized his animals, he hardly ever sentimentalized them as Seton too often did by giving them names (Johnny Bear, Raggylug the cottontail rabbit) and drawing excessively cute pictures to illustrate them. But they were at one in believing that a full understanding of animal ways came from imaginative rapport as well as from scientifically accurate observation, and both believed that they detected rudimentary reason behind animal action just as they observed animal instinct – often leading to violence – close to the surface of human behaviour. Above all, both convey in their different ways a sense of wildness and otherness, of tracts that may seem from a human perspective deserted and barren but are in fact as full of story as the more exclusively human world. In so doing, they introduce us to a realm that provides the background for so many later literary works as diverse as Pratt's 'The Great Feud' and Atwood's *Surfacing*. Despite the urban face of modern Canada, the wilderness still abides as a surrounding presence, and Seton and Roberts found a way of annexing it, hauntingly, imaginatively, to our literature.

There can be no more dramatic illustration of the diversity of Canadian experience at the turn of the nineteenth and twentieth centuries than the fact that Seton and Roberts's stories of wilderness and ancient wood appeared contemporaneously with the polished, sophisticated, politically astute comedies of manners of Sara Jeannette Duncan. Duncan (who married Everard Coates, a civil servant and journalist, lived for most of her subsequent life in India and England, and published many of her novels under her married name) was born in Brantford, Ontario, in 1862, and drew upon her personal memories of small-town life for Elgin, the setting for *The Imperialist* (1904), the novel by which she is best known to Canadians. But she had long since outgrown any possible limitations in her provincial upbringing. She had, for example, clearly and successfully challenged the behavioural norms of Victorian womanhood in her first book, *A Social Departure* (1890), which offered an amusing if excessively flippant account of a trip round the world (mainly to the Middle and Far East) undertaken when she was still in her twenties and accompanied only by a woman fellow journalist.

Duncan was an inveterate traveller, and her first book involves shrewd comparisons between the social customs of one country and another. Although she never achieves the subtlety and penetrating psychological insight of Henry James, she shares with him a serious and deliberate analysis of the international theme. As several of her titles suggest, notably *An American Girl in London* (1891), *Those Delightful Americans* (1902), and *Cousin Cinderella: A Canadian Girl in London* (1908), her basic structures are often similar to his: the protagonist, generally a young woman, is set down in a foreign country and gradually comes to terms with the culture in which she finds herself, attaining a deeper understanding of her own in the process. At various times, Canadians, Americans, English, and East Indians are juxtaposed, along with their respective cultures, in her fiction.

Although many of her novels, especially *Cousin Cinderella*, reveal Duncan's basic Canadian attitudes even when they are set abroad, *The Imperialist* is her main contribution, in terms both of content and of quality, to the Canadian fictional tradition. Nowadays the title inevitably conjures up visions of colonial dependency, and even Kipling's lesser breeds without the law, but Lorne Murchison, Duncan's protagonist, is as much a Canadian nationalist as a British imperialist. His vision, at one with late nineteenth-century imperialist thought, is of a commonwealth federation in which the Dominion of Canada would play a full and perhaps decisive role in international affairs. It implies a role of leadership and influence with no trace of colonial subservience, and developed historically along with increased fears of the economic and cultural dominance of the United States.

At once a comedy of manners and an examination of Canadian-English-American relations, *The Imperialist* is a novel that exists within the extremes of the regional (Elgin and Fox County, Ontario) and the imperialist dream, between the provincial and the cosmopolitan. It is not so much a novel of politics as of human responses to politics. Murchison is an idealist who comes up against harsh realities in both politics and love. Structurally, the book is well balanced, Murchison (though presented as an attractive and often sympathetic figure) losing his girl and his political candidacy at the same time. In addition, a subplot involves his sister Alvina and her love for a newly arrived Scots minister, with complications arising from the latter's prior engagement before coming to Canada. Here, and in Murchison's visit to England as secretary to a governmental deputation, Duncan's international theme is again explored at both social and political levels.

The Imperialist is most remarkable, however, for its tone and style. Duncan here achieves a combination of poise, wit, elegance, and social insight rare in Canadian literature. The opening chapters, which offer Elgin as a microcosm of Canadian society as well as a 'little outpost of empire' (Ch. 2), help to establish the small town as an artistically rich subject for the country's fiction, and the intimate colloquial rhythms of the narrator in passages such as the following must surely have influenced Leacock: 'When you have seen your daughter reach and pass the age of twenty-five without having learned properly to make her own bed, you know without being told that she will never be fit for the management of a house – don't you? Very well then' (Ch. 3). But Duncan goes beyond this. In Elgin she achieves an impressive sense of a living community, and can go on, in her presentation of social distinctions and political liaisons, to show a society in the process of significant development. 'We are here', she notes at one point, 'at the beginning of a nation' (Ch. 5). The confident flow of the narration holds in balance the serious political themes and the comic conventions in which they are imbedded. Moreover, it is a tribute to Duncan's artistic integrity that the logic of the novel severely qualifies, perhaps even undercuts, her own imperialist convictions.

Duncan temporarily established herself as a talented popular writer in England and the United States as well as in Canada. *The Imperialist*, one of her less successful works on first publication, shows her achieving a sustained level of seriousness that she rarely attempted and only fitfully attained in her other books. She remains an accomplished minor novelist in a period when major practitioners were transforming the genre through the development of excitingly original artistic techniques. Elsewhere she is now forgotten, but she brought a critical intelligence, a professional competence, and above all a stylistic sensitivity to Canadian fiction at a time when they were desperately needed. Before her contribution, the novelistic achievement is disappointing, a collection of generally unrelated texts displaying few signs of formal coherence or thematic interconnection. Duncan was not destined to lay any firm foundation for a characteristically Canadian fiction – for that we must await the stolid contribution of Frederick Philip Grove – but she performed an inestimable service at the beginning of the new century by providing a sturdy example and, in *The Imperialist,* setting a new standard of accomplishment.

Part Two

Poetry

Chapter 4

The Challenge of Modernism

E. J. Pratt dominates Canadian poetry in the first half of the twentieth century not merely by virtue of the intrinsic quality of his work but also because of his pivotal position within the history of the country's verse. He provides an essential link between the attitudes and assumptions of the Confederation Poets on the one hand and modernist principles and practice on the other. It took Canadians a long time to come to terms with the poetic revolution of the early twentieth century associated with the names of Ezra Pound and T. S. Eliot. 'To Canada', as the elderly Roberts remarked in 1931, 'modernism has come more slowly and less violently than elsewhere' (*Selected Poetry and Critical Prose*, 1974, 298). There was no rush to emulate the latest poetic fashion; however, Pratt's early verse, colloquial but not obscure, recognizably new but decidedly not newfangled, can now be seen as bridging the gap between the traditional and the contemporary.

Pratt was able to move with comparative ease between the two worlds. A poem like 'The Iron Door' (1927), a dream-vision about the entrance to the world of death, has an earnestly Victorian tone and recalls some of the more visionary and idealistic poems of Roberts and Lampman, but a few years later selections from his work appeared, not too uncomfortably, in *New Provinces* (1936), the historically significant anthology in which A. J. M. Smith, F. R. Scott, and A. M. Klein first published their work in volume form. Like Duncan Campbell Scott, he can be classified as 'Victorian' or 'modern', but his dates (1882–1964) show him to be an intermediate, transitional figure. Nevertheless, although a contemporary of Lawrence, Eliot, and Joyce, he seems older than they because he was more concerned, both intellectually and artistically, with evolution rather than revolution; he was content to develop out of, rather than break away from, the world of nineteenth-century humanism. Thus he accepted Darwin's theory in principle without assuming that it precluded a divine origin, and spent a lifetime probing in verse the relation between Christianity and evolutionary theory. This perspective, which would have seemed curiously old-fashioned in the equivalent literary worlds of Britain and the United States, enabled him paradoxically to present aspects of modern experience of which those self-consciously intent upon keeping to the mainstream knew little or nothing.

His unique position within Canadian poetry can be understood in geographical as well as historical terms. Born in Newfoundland, son of a Methodist minister and grandson of a sea captain, he was brought up in a 'backward' community where folk songs and oral traditions were still strong, where the constant human struggle with the hostile forces of nature was a basic fact of life. He then went to Toronto where he studied arts, philosophy, psychology, and theology. Like his later student and editor, Northrop Frye, he was ordained but, instead of entering the ministry, became a university teacher of English. He spans, therefore, not only the nineteenth and twentieth centuries but the extremes of primitive-rural and sophisticated-urban living.

Pratt's poems are generally about conflict – between man and man, animal and animal, man and natural forces, etc. – and their linguistic vitality reflects a world in which force and energy are paramount. Although he concentrated on heroic action at a time when traditional heroism was an unfashionable quality in higher literary circles, his work can be surprisingly modern. Conversely, while he often wrote about contemporary events (*The Roosevelt and the Antinoe*, 1930; *The Titanic*, 1935; *Dunkirk*, 1941), his contemporaneity is not confined to such material. Pratt works indirectly. 'The Great Feud', a poem about a prehistoric animal struggle, is suddenly recognized as an oblique commentary on 'the years of *l'entre deux guerres*'; an innocent-looking poem about a prize cat is found to end on a bitter allusion to Mussolini's invasion of Ethiopia; the Great Panjandrum in 'The Truant' rules over a mechanical universe but also displays the characteristics of a Hitler. Moreover, Pratt's fascination with detail, both scientific and verbal, that manifests itself in his narrative-cum-documentary poems, reveals him as one of the best qualified of twentieth-century poets to master, and make available for poetry, the technical vocabulary of the modern age. All this enabled him (relatively speaking, of course) to become both popular and, in Frye's words, 'one of our scholarly poets' (*Bush Garden* 182).

His first volume, *Newfoundland Verse*, appeared in 1923. Much of its content is conventional and uninspiring, but the better poems foreshadow his later development. 'Newfoundland' is an example of the meticulous structuring of his shorter poems, as images of

> *Tide and wind and crag,*
> *Sea-weed and sea-shell*
> *And broken rudder*

balance each other from verse to verse. Here is a poetry saturated in the maritime imagery of the eastern seaboard; the tides that 'run / Within the sluices of men's hearts' remind us of similar effects in Roberts (in 'Ave' and 'The Vagrant of Time'), while the movement of the lines, poised between metrical regularity and vers libre, often recall Duncan Campbell Scott. Similarly, 'The Shark' anticipates Pratt's later preoccupations with the coolly ferocious efficiency of wild creatures; the fish is seen in terms of mechanism just as, later, mechanism will be endued metaphorically with the quality of life. Moreover, in 'Carlo', the story of a mongrel who allegedly played a vital part in a sea rescue, we get a first taste of Pratt's colloquial vitality. From the opening couplet, 'I see no use in not confessing – / To trace your breed would keep me guessing', we recognize the accents of a speaking voice that has no patience with the affectedly poetic. The bold, often blatant rhymes, the ebullient humour and unsophisticated good sense, are endearing, and create an effect rarely heard until then in Canadian poetry. Close to the popular verse of McLachlan, Robert Service and Tom MacInnes, it is far more subtly modulated. If it recalls anything, it is the vernacular poetry of Robert Frost – a reminder that, for all Pratt's loyalty to British tradition, his own writing naturally follows a North American cadence.

Pratt soon recognized his special poetic gifts and proceeded to develop them. For example, many of his poems from the 1920s and 1930s explore the origins of humanity and nature from a cosmic perspective. These are excellent examples of originality arising out of tradition. They contemplate 'the wide awe and wisdom of the night' and probe 'beyond the tops of time' (both titles of poems by Roberts), but they do so with imaginative gusto, avoiding any trace of the pretentious. The shorter poems written in lyrical measures are tightly packed, their tone exquisitely controlled. 'From Stone to Steel' is a deservedly well-known example. Pratt ranges from Java to Geneva, from the Euphrates to the Rhine, drawing upon all the implications from archaeology, theology, history, geography, and modern politics associated with these euphonious place names, and the uncertain relation between physical evolution and moral progress is brilliantly caught in concentrated images – when he observes, for instance, how 'The civil polish of the horn / Gleams from our praying finger tips'. Elsewhere the effect is more fanciful but ultimately no less serious. In 'The Highway', the stars in their courses are described in terms of astronomical show business when the cosmic seneschal 'Announced at his high carnival / An orbit – with Aldebaran!'. Such imaginative flights culminate in 'The Truant', in which the name character representing humanity, having evolved a moral consciousness, defies the tyrant god of a mechanistic universe. This is a poem as profound as it is vigorous in which Pratt, while in no way defying religious orthodoxy, claims the freedom to explore other possibilities. He has discovered that, to probe the mysteries of life intelligently, one does not need the sonorous sublimities of a Milton; *The Witches' Brew* (1926) even parodies the cosmology of *Paradise Lost* (see Djwa 44). In 'The Truant', for all the high-spirited clowning about 'flunkey decimals' (l. 96) and 'our kiddy cars of inverse squares' (l. 125), Pratt makes the human defiance of cosmic tyranny moving, dignified, and fundamentally Christian: '"No, *by the Rood*, we will not join your ballet"' [my italics].

Yet, for all the accomplishments of his shorter poems, Pratt enjoyed even greater success with his longer narratives. Though seldom more than a few hundred lines long, these poems achieve, both individually and collectively, an epic breadth. Pratt continually insists that, whatever the intellectual theorists may say, modern life contains just as many opportunities for heroic action as the ancient world. 'The Toll of the Bells', an early poem about contemporary Newfoundland fishermen, celebrates an 'Iliad of Death upon the floes'; the story of *The Titanic* involves

> That ancient *hubris* in the dreams of men,
> Which would have slain the cattle of the sun,
> And filched the lightnings from the fist of Zeus.
>
> (ll. 50–52)

For Pratt the Second World War was no less promising a subject for poetry than the Trojan War. In all these poems ('The Great Feud', set in 'a *Pleistocene Armageddon*', is only superficially an exception, since it presents a nature red in tooth and claw out of which the human race will evolve), his chief hero is humanity. Even in *The Titanic*, where humanity pays for its technological arrogance, the test occurs after the collision, when for the most part individuals demonstrate the dignified self-sacrifice of which the species is capable. Characteristically, however, Pratt presents moral struggle through the metaphor of physical conflict as 'self-preservation fought / Its red primordial struggle with the "ought"' (ll. 991–2).

Brébeuf and His Brethren (1940) and *Towards the Last Spike* (1952), his most ambitious poems that make use of Canadian subject matter, deserve special attention. Pratt was acutely aware of the fact that Canada, as a young country, lacked the epic phase of older cultures, and he duly filled the gap by producing extended treatments of two epic stories – one going back three centuries and involving physical endurance and religious fervour, the other belonging to the more immediate past and exploring a secular, even technological subject. Once again we note Pratt's transitional stance: his emphasis on heroic action appeared old-fashioned, yet we can now recognize him as a precursor of those writers who, within the last forty years, have discovered and re-created the Canadian past in prose and verse.

In *Brébeuf*, Pratt retells the story of the Jesuit missionaries martyred by the Iroquois in 1649. The poem is written in unrhymed verse of impressive force and eloquence, and celebrates both the physical courage and spiritual vision of the name character and his fellow priests. Brébeuf himself is a giant in the true epic mould, yet Pratt chooses to emphasize his greatness of soul, and this is only one of the many subtleties within the poem. Unfortunately, these complexities have too often been misinterpreted, or not recognized, by Pratt's critics. One example, interesting because it shows the extent to which poets younger than Pratt were puzzled by his attitudes, involves F. R. Scott, who wrote a short squib-poem with the same title that ends: 'Then is priest savage or Red Indian priest?' Scott implies that Pratt was unaware of the interconnection between his two sets of protagonists, that he presents the story in simplistic hero/villain terms. Yet Pratt's title itself alerts us to the human identification within the poem. He knows that all men are brothers, that Brébeuf's 'brethren' are the Iroquois as well as his fellow Jesuits. The poet admires the heroic qualities of both pagans and Christians (without, of course, equating their positions in moral terms). Brébeuf is no less sympathetic a character, and no less a Christian, because Pratt is fascinated by the combination of god-like devotion and all-too-human pride in his make-up. While the narrative is both historically accurate and a rousing story of adventure and suffering, it offers profound insights into the complex nature of humanity.

Whereas *Brébeuf* is epic tragedy, *Towards the Last Spike,* no less epic in conception, conforms to the pattern of comedy. It is a story of challenge and ultimate triumph. The building of a transcontinental railway may seem at first sight an unpromising subject for poetry, but in it Pratt recognized a uniquely Canadian epic subject. Not only does it contain the story of the unification of the country, but its concentration on technological development and above all on the centrality of communications gives it a distinct sense of modernity. The old subject of humanity versus nature appears in new guise. As usual, Pratt stresses the heroic splendour of the achievement, but alongside the physical struggle is another in which the battlefield is Parliament, the weapons words and rhetoric: Sir John A. Macdonald's *'from sea to sea'* (l. 552) against Edward Blake's doubting '*To build a road over that sea of mountains*' (l. 535). The poem is about both the image of union and the union of images; the subject of communication is underpinned by continuing similes and metaphors drawn from grammar and speech. Once again, Pratt encountered criticism. 'Where are the coolies in your poem, Ned?' asked Scott in another satirical squib ('All Spikes But the Last'), yet again the arrow lands off target. Pratt understands the contribution of ordinary labour, native or imported, but he also knows that the scheme required not only sweat and muscle but vision; and it is this imaginative vision (by no means unrelated to Brébeuf's) that is celebrated here.

In the end 'the breed had triumphed after all' (l. 1622). Much has been written about Pratt, individualism, and 'corporate man'; it seems fair to conclude that Pratt celebrated the individual hero, the strong man endowed with determination, physical strength, and the all-important vision, yet realized that he could only operate within a social context or a like-minded group. The leader depends upon the led, but Pratt never forgot that the led also depend upon a leader. In the history of Canadian poetry Pratt himself was a leader, and he excels through the sheer bulk, variety, and energy of his words. His epic lists, each word rolled lovingly round the tongue, are famous. He is one of those word-obsessed poets (Irving Layton is another) who cannot be properly read without a dictionary close at hand. But it is Pratt's *joy* in words that ultimately distinguished him. He loves them, loves to mould and arrange them, and thereby comes to control them. The Confederation Poets used words, often very effectively, but they rarely dominated them. Pratt brought into Canadian poetry a much-needed awareness of the power and possibility inherent in language. However much he may have differed in beliefs, preferences, cast of mind, from those who came after him, Pratt's emphasis on verbal energy (which went hand in hand with verbal precision) has put all subsequent Canadian poets in his debt.

Although he published little of note until 1923, Pratt had grown to maturity in the years preceding the First World War. He found his own highly individualistic solution to the gap that had opened up between Victorian assumptions and the experiences of the twentieth century, but his example was not one that others could easily follow. The world had changed drastically, but the established Canadian poets (Roberts, Carman, even Duncan Campbell Scott) went on in much the same way. Until the 1930s Canada saw little of the artistic challenge and achievement of the modernist movement that had transformed literary attitudes in other parts of the English-speaking world. But during the 1920s W. W. E. Ross and Raymond Knister, two talented younger writers more in tune with contemporary developments elsewhere, were conducting private experiments in poetic diction and rhythm. Both were at first rejected by their own country and had to publish in poetry magazines abroad (the United States and also, in Knister's case, Paris). The output of both is quantitatively small and qualitatively uneven, but they provided an essential first step.

Ross has been hailed by Raymond Souster as 'the first important modern Canadian poet writing in English' (preface to Ross, *Experiment 1923–9*, 1956, 23). Though he produced both experimental and highly traditional verse, he is remembered for his own particular brand of Imagism. Trained as a scientist, he had learned to keep his eye firmly on the object. Instead of recording his thoughts and emotions he presented what he saw in short lines, without verbal decoration, as simply as possible. For example:

> The dawn; the birds'
> tumultuous clamour
> grows as the light
> gradually makes
> more distinct
> the rocks, the trees,
> picking out each
> from among the grey.

('The Dawn; the Birds'')

And:

> Down by the
> shore hangs a
> branch of the
> pale-stemmed
> trembling-leafed
> poplar.

('By the Shore')

Often Ross wrote of the northern Ontario scenery that was providing favourite subjects for the Group of Seven, and his poems sometimes seem like verbal equivalents of these paintings. There is a bold clarity about both his observations and his language. In general he eschews metaphor, thus paralleling in verse the straightforward directness that Morley Callaghan was at the same time developing in Canadian fictional prose.

Ross is, then, of special interest because his poetic experimentation connects with an attempt to distinguish not only a Canadian subject matter but a characteristically Canadian style. In his verse foreword to *Laconics* (1929) he expresses the need to isolate 'what quality may mark us off / from older Europe' and hopes that his poetry will contain 'the sharper tang of Canada'. He acknowledged Marianne Moore and E. E. Cummings (but not, it is interesting to note, Pound or William Carlos Williams) as masters who inspired if not influenced him, and he was clearly seeking an alternative to regular syllabic verse. At the same time – and this perhaps distinguishes the Canadian experiment from the larger North American context – he was loath to cut all links with 'older Europe'. Thus the first extract quoted in the previous paragraph is obviously moving in the direction of vers libre. The second, however, if read as a single line with a caesura after 'branch', is seen to look back to the classical hexameter, and this is true of a surprising number of his apparently irregular poems. Ross was experimental though by no means revolutionary in his literary aims, but he saw clearly that a distinctively Canadian poetry had to be founded on an equally distinctive way of employing words and rhythms.

Raymond Knister, who died young before fulfilling his early promise, came from a rural background, and most of his poems, like his short stories, are set in farm and countryside. His interests and temperament were close to Lampman's, but Knister wrote as a participator in the scenes that he portrayed. The poems arise from within the landscape and are rarely imposed upon it. His approach to poetry is well summed up in a foreword he wrote for a projected volume of selected poems: 'Birds and flowers and dreams are real as sweating men and swilling pigs. But the feeling about them is not always so real, any more, when it gets into words' (*Collected Poems* 7). His verse is often more consciously eloquent than Ross's – 'This is April, and the sumach candles / Have guttered long ago' ('Boy Remembers in the Field') – but he shows the same capacity to find the quintessential image to convey a larger scene, as in the following vignette of a farmer sowing;

> Shoes dragging the clods,
> Eyes busy;
> Arm-weight hanging limply
> To the lines ...
>
> ('In the Rain, Sowing Oats')

Knister was learning his craft at the same time that he was experimenting with new techniques. We do not find the same sense of achieved purpose that is evident in Ross's work. Too often Knister gives the impression of not quite succeeding in what he attempts. His rhythms are discontinuous; lines tend to lapse into that unsatisfactory no man's land between verse and prose. His strength is that, at his best, he did not extrapolate from his immediate experience. A particular moment is rarely generalized or made representative – it's simply there. His was a fragile talent, but he frequently achieved an impressionistic vividness in such lines as

> Across pasture, through a surf of golden-rod
> Boys wade; Sunday,
> And there may be mushrooms.
>
> ('After Exile')

This promised to become the hallmark of a mature style that he never lived to perfect.

But the main impetus in bringing Canadian poetry into the twentieth century came from the so-called 'McGill Movement' led by A. J. M. Smith with the assistance of F. R. Scott, and involving A. M. Klein (of whom more later), Leo Kennedy, and Leon Edel. Smith, though beginning his undergraduate career as a science student, was widely read in the new poetry of Eliot, Yeats, and Pound, and was distressed to discover a lack of technical and intellectual seriousness among contemporary Canadian poets. In 1925 Smith and Scott founded the *McGill Fortnightly Review* to campaign for modernism in Canada, and the next few years saw a lively succession of articles and verse, here and in other magazines such as the *Canadian Forum*, advocating or exemplifying the need for more rigorous standards of excellence in both poetry and literary criticism. 'Poetry today,' Smith wrote, 'must be the result of the impingement of modern conditions upon the personality and temperament of the poet' (qtd. in Dudek and Gnarowski 28). He advocated respect for poetic craftsmanship, the fusion of thought and feeling, the exercise of critical intelligence ('poetry is more concerned with expressing exact ideas than wishy-washy "dreams"' [ibid. 41]), and, above all, precise diction – 'words / As crisp and as white / As our snow' ('To Hold in a Poem'). Moreover, at this period and in his later career as 'compulsive anthologist' (Smith's anthologies, especially *The Book of Canadian Poetry,* 1943, have been of incalculable importance in establishing a Canadian poetic tradition), he steadfastly protested against the various forms of narrowness that manifest themselves in Canada as puritanism, provincialism, and colonialism.

It is easy today to observe that the importation of international modernism into Canada could itself be seen as an example of the deferential colonialism that Smith claimed to oppose. His support of the 'cosmopolitan' over the 'native' has often been criticized, but the native against which he rebelled was not the achievement represented by (say) Lampman, Duncan Campbell Scott, and Pratt but the maple-and-beaver references of a self-conscious pseudo-nationalism. His complaint was not so much that Canada was a backwater as that the backwater in question was stagnant and needed revivification through contact with fresher and more vigorous streams. Smith, as his later criticism makes clear, did not want Canadian poets to imitate Eliot and the moderns but rather to attain an equivalent standard and importance. The literary efflorescence that Canada began to enjoy in the 1940s has produced many writers who disagree with Smith's artistic preferences, but they could hardly have succeeded without the energy and determination of Smith's literary leadership in earlier years.

Present-day readers of Smith's own poetry will immediately be struck by the emphasis on art and artifice, which extends well beyond the frequent references, direct or indirect, to other writers and their work. The poems are offered as exquisitely finished objects, like classical statuary that we walk around to appreciate from all angles. We are invited not merely to comprehend the meaning but to admire, and even rejoice in, the successful making. They are poised, witty and eloquent, encompassing a wide range of tone from the comic and familiar through the formal and celebratory to a poetry of grand statement in which personal urgency generally manifests itself within a conscious and unashamed traditionalism. Smith borrows freely from the idiom of past centuries (generally a master of pastiche, he occasionally succumbs to it), and assumes a cultivated audience well versed in the history and achievements of Western culture. Northrop Frye's insistence that poems are made out of other poems applies nowhere more obviously than here. Smith can be as allusive as Eliot, but in the process displays an intellectual exuberance that spills over on to the often bemused but generally stimulated reader. If some of his poems ('The Plot against Proteus', 'Prothalamium', 'The Wisdom of Old Jelly Roll') give the impression of being intellectual puzzles, there is a compelling fascination in the rhetoric that prods us into attempting to follow the quirkish movements of Smith's mind, and they are invariably found to have a serious and legitimate purpose. This side of Smith's art – a curious combination of Eliot-like classicism and Yeatsian romanticism – is indeed 'cosmopolitan', and makes an ambitious bid to exist within the artifice of eternity. Smith is preoccupied with the permanence of art, and takes care that his work is made to last. In 'To a Young Poet' he stresses above all else 'the worth of a thing done / Perfectly, as though without care'.

But there is another side to Smith's poetry which is decidedly 'native' both in reference and in tone. Several imagistic poems recall the work of Ross (to whom 'Wild Raspberry' is dedicated), and his much-discussed preoccupation with hardness, sharpness, and crispness, though evident before Ross began to publish, may not be unrelated to the older poet's 'sharper tang of Canada'. 'The Lonely Land' is deservedly his best-known poem not so much because it offers an unforgettable verbal impression of the northern Canadian landscape but rather because it represents a triumph of subtly controlled vocabulary and carefully modulated rhythms. To call it descriptive would be absurd, since it is primarily a poet's creation:

> This is a beauty
> of dissonance,
> this resonance
> of stony strand …

Smith's verse, with its combination of vivid directness and smooth formality, has also a dissonant beauty; moreover, 'resonance' is a characteristic of his own diction which has won the approval of a poet as unlike Smith as Irving Layton (*Engagements* 76). The fineness of Smith's sensibility has irritated those who consider the vitality of Canadian literature to be dependent upon a North American crude strength. But Smith, while opposed to the outmoded conventions of a tired poetry no longer 'vitally concerned with real experience' (qtd. in Dudek and Gnarowski 39), had no intention of adopting a barbaric yawp. His importance lies in his demonstration of one way in which Canadian poetry could be revived and strengthened by an infusion of vigour and rigour from abroad. His own poetry, excellent within its own boundaries but limited by the lack of a unifying intellectual centre, should be seen as one way among many of fostering an abiding national literature.

F. R. Scott might fairly be described as a complementary opposite to Smith, and his poetry reflects the essential differences in his temperament. A prominent lawyer, defender of civil rights, and tireless campaigner for a moderate and orderly socialism, Scott was far more directly concerned with social and political affairs than Smith; his is noticeably a public poetry – there are no glimpses of an ivory tower as there sometimes are in Smith – and a much larger proportion of his poetic output is devoted to satirical commentary on current affairs. In consequence, he is more consciously nationalistic in his verse, although he would not see this as in any way incompatible with 'cosmopolitan' or international concerns. Finally, while Smith was attracted to art through its promise of permanence, Scott was more immediately conscious of process, of the forces of change at work both in the physical world and in human institutions.

Although Scott had come under the influence of a form of Christian socialism while at Oxford between 1920 and 1923, his early poems are characterized by a tender lyricism which is delightful but limited. It was the influence of Smith that enabled him to broaden his poetic horizons without losing the precision and clarity that his language had always displayed; but it was the economic conditions of the Depression that impelled him to put his poetic gifts to the cause of social and political reform. This satirical poetry has become well known, perhaps because it is a kind of verse comparatively rare in Canada, but it does not, I think, constitute his most lasting work. Like most socially committed literature, it tends to fade with time as its immediate relevance passes. We may well sympathize with the sentiments expressed, but often the targets – big business, political ineptitude, bourgeois snobbery – seem too large and too easy. Sometimes, indeed, the plan can backfire. One wonders, for instance, whether R. B. Bennett and his like bore much resemblance to the straw man portrayed in 'Ode to a Politician'. Even his literary squibs (see pp. 87 –88), though satisfying to the like-minded, are not guaranteed to persuade the unconvinced. The best of his satires, 'The Canadian Authors Meet' and the even wittier but less familiar 'Saturday Sundae', owe their effectiveness less to the subjects parodied than to the verbal skill and exuberance of the poet. When in the former he presents 'Virgins of sixty who still write of passion' or in the latter sums up a whole generation with the lines 'My brothers and my sisters, two by two, / Sit supping succulence and sighing sex', we accept the criticism because we respond to the artistry.

Scott's introspective poetry, which promises to wear extremely well, shows more obvious links with earlier Canadian poetic tradition. More consciously nationalistic than his other writings, this does not mean, of course, that it is superficially patriotic. Scott makes no attempt to 'paint the native maple' with the 'Canadian Authors'. But in poems such as 'Surfaces', 'North Stream', and 'Laurentian Shield', he presents the geological determinants that have created the Canadian land – and, in 'Mount Royal', those that will also destroy it:

> Pay taxes now,
> Elect your boys, lay out your pleasant parks,
> You gill-lunged, quarrelsome ephemera!
> The tension tightens yearly, underneath,
> A folding continent shifts silently
> And oceans wait their turn for snow or streets.

These lines contain the essential Scott. They begin in social sarcasm, but transcend the narrowly political by setting contemporary human actions against the larger movements of cosmological process (a perspective which may owe something to Pratt, with whom Scott frequently argued). Scott has absorbed the findings of modern science, but he remains, politically and spiritually, a visionary. He habitually sees (and words like 'see', 'sight', and 'vision' are central to his work) beyond the superficialities of natural landscape and human behaviour to larger patterns and concepts:

> always we find
> Such ordered purpose in cell and galaxy,
> So great a glory in life-thrust and mind-range.
>
> ('A Grain of Rice')

Thus 'Lakeshore', for Scott, is not an excuse for a description packed with Canadian content, but a profound meditation on humanity 'poised in a still of gravity' between sea and air, past and future. Deeply intellectual without ever sounding dryly academic, Scott brings thought, feeling, wit, and verbal dexterity into all his best work. As Munro Beattie wrote, 'the informed mind has been perfectly co-ordinated with the civilized heart' (LHC II 244).

Dorothy Livesay had been a distinct presence within Canadian poetry from the 1930s, but it was only with the publication of *Collected Poems: The Two Seasons* (1972) that her full stature became apparent. In the foreword to that book she describes her poems as creating 'a psychic if not a literal autobiography', and the impress of her own personality as she chronicles intensely private experience, together with her energetic responses to external events, provides the kind of unifying centre to her work that is lacking in Smith's. 'I live in what I feel and hear / And see', she remarks in 'The Garden of Love', and she is untouched by the modernist craving for impersonality. Although one can attempt a division between her intimate personal poems ('Ballad of Me') and those addressing themselves to social and political issues ('After Hiroshima'), ultimately they all fall into place as individual entries within a lifelong verse diary.

With Livesay, then, it is best to proceed chronologically. Her first book, *Green Pitcher*, appeared as early as 1928, while she was still an undergraduate at the University of Toronto, and we find here the beginnings of the personal lyricism that distinguishes all her work. These are simple, direct poems, not unlike those that Ross and Knister were writing at the same time.

> Over the wood the rain came running
> Like a swift greyhound.
> The dry leaves rustled at the touch of her feet.
>
> ('Shower')

There is an engaging freshness about this, a 'sharp clarity' ('Fire and Reason'), to use a phrase that suggests Smith and is evidence of the spontaneous links between Canadian poets that emerged in the 1920s. All this is a welcome relief from the high-flown solemnities of many of their predecessors. Moreover, we also find, here and in *Signpost* (1932), a persistent use of refrain, of rhetorical and syntactical repetitions often taking the place of rhyme and regular metre, that shows the extent to which her poetry is related to the sanctioned conventions of ballad and song.

After graduation, Livesay went to the University of the Sorbonne to write a thesis on 'Symbolism and the Metaphysical Tradition in English Poetry', and might well have developed into one more traditional but 'cosmopolitan' academic poet. The Depression intervened, however, and instead she became actively engaged in social work and left-wing politics. Suppressing her personal idiom, she turned her attention to a committed, political verse which is, for the most part, too propagandistic in subject and too strident in tone: 'Our silence and the onrush of our feet / Will shout for us: the International's born!' ('In Green Solariums'); 'In Cuba the masses have not blundered! / In Cuba the masses know their foe!' ('Montreal: 1935'). But the much reprinted 'Day and Night', although uneven, displays a genuine power, especially in its command of the particularities of factory labour. In its juxtaposition of the poet's sympathetic commentary with the rhythmic beats of workers' songs –

> One step forward
> Two steps back
> Shove the lever,
> Push it back –

we detect, evident though not yet resolved, that 'pull between community and private identity' which Livesay describes in the foreword to *Collected Poems* as 'characteristic of being a woman' (v) but which is just as surely the mark of being fully human.

'Day and Night' is important, however, for another reason. Like 'Depression Suite' and several other poems of the 1930s, it consists of a series of short poems combined into a larger unity. The answer to the personal challenge of the long poem (one which Klein was also developing at this time) provided Livesay with a means of combining her lyrical gifts with her desire for a more extended form than lyric normally allows. It leads eventually to 'documentaries', which are based, as she says, 'on topical data but held together by descriptive, lyrical, and didactic elements' (Mandel ed., *Contexts* 269). This was a genre which Livesay was the first to isolate and name, and it has proved influential. An excellent example is 'London Revisited: 1946' where the personal response and the generalized experience of the war-battered city are subtly blended. An extension of this form is to be found in 'Prophet of the New World', a poem for voices about the enigmatic figure of Louis Riel, and 'Call My People Home', a radio play in verse on the forced evacuation of Japanese Canadians from British Columbia after Pearl Harbor. In both an artistic balance is achieved between the poet's sympathies and her socio-political principles.

After the 1930s, Livesay's active political commitment lessened. Now a wife and mother, she had deeper human insights to transmute into poetry and began to move, not back to her earlier style, but forward to a new though related poetry of mature experience (innocence and experience are the 'two seasons' of her title). She had always reproduced the authentic rhythms of an individual voice. The 'I' of the poem is continually speaking to 'you' – often, indeed, creating the illusion that the reader is being addressed personally: 'The many blinds we draw, / You and I …' ('Fire and Reason'); 'What is there about you that shakes me / With such sharp coldness …?' ('"Ask of the Winds"'). These are early examples; in the later poetry, the rapport between poet and reader is even more pronounced. It is as if we overhear the most intimate whispered yearnings:

> The woman I am
> is not what you see
> move over love
> make room for me.
>
> ('The Unquiet Bed')

Or:

> I lay all night
> and you not with me
> but you came beside me
> from the dream's distance.
>
> ('The Vigil')

The poems of the 1960s, written after the death of her husband and what must have been a tumultuous adjustment to a new lifestyle, have so poignant a directness, are so nakedly confessional, that we almost feel that we are violating a privacy in reading them. In these remarkable poems about the painful joys and joyful pains of sexual love, Livesay achieves an openness that may be startling but is also deeply moving. Such poems as 'The Touching', 'And Give Us Our Trespasses', and 'The Notations of Love' (all poem sequences) come closer, perhaps, than anything else in Canadian literature to an expression of D. H. Lawrence's sexual tenderness.

Dorothy Livesay is a poet who quietly but resolutely went her own way, avoiding the lures of poetic fashion or artistic theory, but benefiting from contemporary trends when they happened to coincide with the lines of her own development. Her early poems, as I have shown, establish links with the poetry of her own generation, but (with the exception of her political verse) we never suspect that she is conforming to a poetic programme. She was always independent enough to choose the style – however traditional, however avant-garde – that best suited her particular needs at the particular moment. Again, she could not have established her early poems (not, at least, in Canada) before the 'permissive' era of the late 1960s, yet they are obviously written out of a personal compulsion without any idea of exploiting a promising new market. There is no hint of self-indulgence at one extreme nor of an urge to shock the bourgeois on the other. She is one of the most honest writers that Canada has produced, and this means that she readily reveals her weaknesses as well as her strengths. Under the force of emotion she is often led to risk sentimentality, though she almost always skirts it. In her poetry the heart always takes precedence over the head, and she will sometimes confuse the genuineness of an experience with its successful expression. Her weakest poems are generally those that argue a position, her strongest those that articulate a basic response. Some of her later poetry verges on obscurity because it seems *too* private: readers must interpret enigmatic fragments, and are often left uncertain about the precise connections. Yet this is a small price to pay for a body of work that has much to tell us about women and about love. As yet, surprisingly little literary-critical attention has been paid to her verse, perhaps because she is difficult to categorize and because traditional criticism is notoriously ill at ease with the frank expression of passionate emotion. But the complexities of her lyricism demand attention, and in the future she will doubtless receive it.

A. M. Klein is among the earliest and most distinguished of the many

Canadians from neither English nor French backgrounds who have enriched the country's literature with revivifying infusions from their respective cultures. Nevertheless, Klein protested against being categorized as a Jewish poet, and it is easy to understand why: no writers want to be remembered more for their ethnic origins or their favoured subject matter than for the intrinsic quality of their work. At the same time, Klein both flaunted his Jewishness – his first volume, entitled *Hath Not a Jew …* (1940), deliberately excludes all his non-Jewish poems – and spent a lifetime supporting Jewish and Zionist causes. But he never wrote in either Hebrew or Yiddish; his success as a poet is inseparably bound to the English language.

The extraordinary energetic enthusiasm that emanates from his poems arises, I believe, from the creative collision within his mind between the vast collections of stories, customs, and learning that made up his Jewish heritage and a developed and flexible language that had never been used to contain them. The 'tall tales about the Baal Shem Tov' ('Autobiographical') which his father told him as bedtime stories, for instance, were well known within his own culture, and it must have been a shock, but also an exhilarating challenge, to realize that they were virtually unknown to most educated Canadians. Moreover, Klein was acutely conscious of the possibility that North Americanized Jews might lose both their language and their heritage through assimilation; this could be at least partly offset if these stories and traditions were re-created in English. Hence, I think, the emergence of such poems (or, rather, poem sequences) as 'Portraits of a Minyan,' 'Haggadah', 'Of Kith and Kin', 'Of Sundry Folk', and 'Of Holy Vessels'. Here and in more complex ways – in the superb meditation on Spinoza, 'Out of the Pulver and the Polished Lens,' and that terrifying presentation of the Jews as perennial victims, 'Design for Mediaeval Tapestry' – Klein interprets the experience of his own people both to themselves and to others.

For Klein, then, the English language was a precious jar into which might be poured the rich wine of the Jewish tradition. We can see in his early poems an irrepressible revelling in the possibilities of English sounds and rhythms. His verse is studded with archaisms, allusions to the classic English poets, from Chaucer and the Elizabethans onwards, and includes re-creations of earlier styles, as in his parody of Keats's 'La Belle Dame Sans Merci' and especially in 'Childe Harold's Pilgrimage', where a composite 'Wandering Jew' refugee is the speaker:

Of yore yclept in old Judea Zvi;
Cognomen'd Cerf where Latin speech is carolled;
Dubbed Hirsch, a transient, in wild Allmany,
For sweet conformity now appellated Harold ...

Here (in an admittedly extreme example) we are confronted with the crucial problem of Klein's language. Who else would dare to employ such
verbose effects in the twentieth century? Can parody, pastiche, or mere
verbal high spirits justify it? How seriously was it intended? How true is it
to say, with Dudek, that Klein 'spoiled his language with rhetoric'
(*Selected Essays* 101)?

The references to Keats and Byron reveal the essentially Romantic
basis to Klein's personality. His 'O's and 'Dost thou's may well disturb us,
though only the most austerely classical can wholly resist the infectious
zest of his love affair with the English language. And we may well recall at
this point (a poem like 'Legend of Lebanon' may help) that part of Klein's
tradition comes to us through the King James Version of the Old Testament, and that his style derives not merely from the poets of European
romanticism but from the Hebrew tradition that finds its supreme
expression in the Psalms (Klein was to produce his own psalms) and the
Song of Songs. The boy in the Montréal 'ghetto' who 'Dreamed
pavement into pleasant Bible-land' grew into the adult who still sought 'a
fabled city' standing 'in Space's vapours and Time's haze' ('Autobiographical'). Klein's visionary imagination, attuned to both the Romantics
and the Hebrew prophets, was at the same time his curse and his glory.

Klein's love of language led naturally to a delight in verbal effects of
all kinds. An inveterate punster, he would play on any word, especially his
own name (his poetry is riddled with self-deprecating references to a 'little' Jew). It also led to a fascination with Joyce, for whose *Ulysses* (not,
interestingly, *Finnegans Wake*) he intended to provide a sort of secular
Talmud. This is no mere rhetorical flourish on my part. Klein spent years
working on a never-to-be-completed commentary on the allusions in
Ulysses, that was intended to be as comprehensive and subtle as any
exegesis of holy writ. He was partly attracted, of course, by Joyce's Jewish
hero, but more, one suspects, by the combination of seriousness and

humour in his approach to words and meanings. If mention of Joyce, however, suggests an allegiance to the fountainhead of modernism, Klein was in other ways profoundly traditionalist. Thus he needed the rhythms and effect of poetic convention; no verse, for him, could ever be free. Nor was he impressed by modernist theories about plain speech and the use of the vernacular – his verse is filled with the poeticisms that were anathema to Pound. He seems to have loved *all* language, and made no linguistic distinctions between the antique and the contemporary.

As might be expected, he shows few signs of being aware of earlier Canadian writing in English, though *The Hitleriad* (1944), an eloquently vituperative attack on the anti-Semitism of the Third Reich, may owe some of its rhythmic vitality to Pratt's example. But Klein's 'tradition' (and this links him not only with later Jewish-Canadian writers but with representatives of other cultures such as Rudy Wiebe) is not the tradition of a large section of his readers, who may well be bemused when confronted with such titles as 'Reb Levi Yitschok Talks to God' or 'Yehudi Halevi: His Pilgrimage'. True, his Gentile readers may be comforted in part by the knowledge that Klein's encyclopedic learning makes many of his references equally obscure to his own people, but the difficulty inherent in his material is another example of a curse that is also a blessing. T. S. Eliot's famous remark about the ability of poetry to communicate before it is totally understood is applicable here. Klein's verse offers a subtle insight into what it means, for a man of intellect and sensibility, to inherit the wonder and the burden of the Jewish past. This involves conveying a sense of mystery, of customs and references accepted but not fully comprehended. Part of the effect depends upon the way in which we are gradually, with a combination of faith in the poet and awe at the splendour of his heritage, drawn into an unfamiliar world that is simultaneously new and as old as time.

But Klein's last volume of verse, *The Rocking Chair* (1948), moves into a different tradition, since it is distinguished by a preoccupation with French Canada, with its people and its way of life. Obviously – Klein said as much himself, and the point is made by all commentators – he is now turning his attentions to another ethnic minority, presenting their experience and heritage in a varied but unified series of poetic tableaux (the sequence has here expanded to comprise the whole book). This principle of difference within sameness (or vice versa) operates in several ways.

Each poem takes a traditional subject from Québécois life (Catholic piety in 'The Cripples', traditional rural pursuits in 'The Sugaring', a symbolic object in 'The Rocking Chair' and 'The Spinning Wheel,' representative human types in 'M. Bertrand' and 'Monsieur Gaston', and various vignettes of politics, scenery, the city of Montréal, etc.). Readers of the book take away from it the acute sense of a culture in much the same way as in his Jewish work.

And connecting all is Klein's conspicuous, often excessive, but hauntingly memorable style, well illustrated by the opening lines of 'The Snowshoers':

> The jolly icicles ringing in their throats,
> their mouths meerschaums of vapour,
> from the saints' parishes they come, like snowmen
> spangled, with spectrum colour
> patching the scarf green, sash red, sky-blue the coat –
> come to the crystal course.

As always, Klein has a gift for the resonant line. The ordinary is made extraordinary through the polished lens of his language. Sometimes it creates a surprisingly personal effect as in the well-known closing lines of 'The Cripples' which chronicle Klein's lapse from orthodoxy (but not, be it noted, from deeply religious convictions):

> And I who in my own faith once had faith like this,
> but have not now, am crippled more than they.

Sometimes a single word lights up surprising interconnections, as in 'Indian Reservation: Caughnawaga' with its passionately bitter description of the Indian situation as seen through centuries of Jewish experience:

> This is a grassy ghetto, and no home.
> And these are fauna in a museum kept.
> The better hunters have prevailed.

And sometimes there is the ebullient excess of verbal pyrotechnics reminiscent of Joyce, as in 'Montreal', which Klein claimed to be comprehensible to both English and French monoglots, and in which he celebrates the city's linguistic complexity:

> Where English vocable and roll Ecossic
> Mollified by the parle of French
> Bilinguefact your air!

Klein is a prominent but enigmatic figure within the history of Canadian poetry. Somewhat younger than Smith and Scott, he nevertheless attended McGill at the same time; but he was only peripherally associated with the McGill Movement and never appeared in the *McGill Fortnightly Review*. Somewhat older than most of the Montréal poets who founded the rival poetry magazines *Preview* and *First Statement* in 1942, he avoided taking sides and published in both. He preferred to be independent of cliques, but that is only part of the story. Psychologically he was 'solitary man'. The last poem in *The Rocking Chair*, 'Portrait of the Poet as Landscape', shows clearly the fatal split between blessing and curse, the archetype of Romanticism, still haunting him. 'The poet' (Klein, of course) can be 'the nth Adam taking a green inventory / in world but scarcely uttered', yet in another mood 'Sometimes, reduced to nadir, he will think all lost'. The poem aptly chronicles his artistic loneliness. Unfortunately, the latter mood gained ascendancy, and the poem poignantly anticipates the mental breakdown that led to the tragic withdrawal of his last years. But between the youthful linguistic excesses and that final silence exists an achieved body of work of permanent value, an original poetic synthesis created out of his rich cultural heritage and his multifaceted personal experience.

Earle Birney is well known as the author of 'David', but even the most superficial perusal of his verse reveals that this is an inadequate designation. It is difficult, however, to generalize about his poems since they vary so much in subject, tone, and treatment, as well as in quality. They may be narratives, dramatic monologues, lyrics; they may be brooding, satirical, hilarious. We recognize rich diversity rather than single-minded consistency of approach. Birney's is essentially a poetry of process, of responses to the moment that do not necessarily blend with the responses of the past and may well be supplanted or contradicted in the future. Like Livesay's, his *Collected Poems* (1975) give the impression of a verse diary, but a diary of observations and attitudes rather than of intimate personal experience; a large proportion is given up to impressions of his travels both in Canada and abroad, but the man himself remains surprisingly elusive.

Nevertheless, although the emphasis generally falls on the poem rather than the poet, we detect two almost irreconcilable Birneys, or personae for Birney, at the extremes of the spectrum: a dour but stoic pessimist anticipating the imminent destruction of humanity, and (particularly in his later years) an irrepressible buffoon, playful, punning, ebullient, fond of verbal doodling that results in what he calls in one of his book titles *Pnomes Jukollages & Other Stunzas* (1969). The two are not in fact as opposed as they might seem. The gloom and doom of the former is qualified and heightened by the energy and skill of the language through which it is filtered, and the apparently lighthearted and iconoclastic joke-poems often reveal a serious purpose under the verbal and typographical clowning. I agree with George Woodcock, however, that Birney's more radical verse/experiments 'should perhaps be classed as "entertainments" rather than as "poems" to distinguish them from works of the calibre of "David" and "November Walk" and "Cartagena de Indias," which have no need of whimsical adornments to wreak their profound effects' (*World* 100). Birney is a contemporary of Smith, F. R. Scott, and Klein, but he came into prominence later than they, and belongs to a later stage in the development of Canadian poetry. Just as Pratt provided an important link between the Confederation Poets and the early modernists, so Birney spans the period between Pratt and the younger experimentalists of the 1960s. When 'David' first appeared in volume form (1942), Pratt praised it for possessing 'the strength and stride of good narrative' (Nesbitt ed., 41), and we recognize here a quality Birney shares with the author of 'The Cachalot' and *The Titanic*. Other qualities in 'David' also recall Pratt: the presentation of humanity pitting itself against the harsh and relentless challenge of the natural world; the introduction of highly technical vocabulary; the emphasis on courage, loyalty, and defiance that Birney himself admired in the older poet (Smith ed., *Masks*, 1962, 90). On the other hand, if we turn to a late Birney poem, 'Fall by Fury' (1978), although we find much to remind us of 'David' – both poems involve climbing accidents and variations on the theme of hubris – we are just as clearly in the poetic world of Al Purdy. 'David' is a distanced narrative (the 'I' is not Birney), written in an intricate stanza pattern with internal and half rhymes, and thus tightly controlled; 'Fall by Fury', a highly individual anecdote told in the poet's first person, is superficially irregular (though disciplined by alliteration, assonance, and emphatic accentual beats), and thus gives the illusion of being both spontaneous and relaxed.

Historically, Birney is important within Canadian poetry as the first poet of any consequence to be born west of Ontario, and the first to embody the western experience in his verse. 'David' is, of course, a classic of the Rockies, but other poems such as 'Vancouver Lights', 'Dusk on English Bay', 'November Walk Near False Creek Mouth', not to mention his play *The Damnation of Vancouver* (the original title of *Trial of a City*, 1952), all advertise, in their titles, his sense of a specific western topography. Still others, like 'Bushed' and 'The Mammoth Corridors', could hardly have been written without a personal saturation in the unique configurations of western place and time. Ironically, Birney is nudged into his most characteristically Canadian poems by the fact that Canada's most 'British' settlements exist on the edge of the Pacific, where

> the barren end of the ancient English
> who tippled mead in Alfred's hall
> and took tiffin in lost Lahore
> drink now their fouroclock chainstore tea
> sighing like pines as the wind turns.
>
> ('November Walk ...', ll. 8–12)

He knows, none better, that 'there is no clear Strait of Anian / to lead us easy back to Europe' ('Pacific Door'), yet he also knows (he was for many years a university teacher of Old and Middle English) that the grainy texture of his verse rhythms derives from the Anglo-Saxon poetic craft also fostered in 'Alfred's hall'. Birney's originality, which is paramount, expresses itself within the discipline and challenge of a cultural tradition inherent in the history of the English language.

Originality and tradition come together in many of the poems already mentioned, and in others such as 'The Wind through Saint

John's', founded upon a recurrent Birney situation: the solitary poet looking out from a threatened civilization towards what Matthew Arnold
called 'the unplumb'd salt, estranging sea' and Birney, in 'Pacific Door',
calls 'the simple unhuman truth of this emptiness'. The situation is that of
the speakers in the Old English 'Seafarer' and 'Wanderer' poems; in
'Mappemounde', as everyone points out, Birney combines both the tone
and the verse-form of the Anglo-Saxons. But an important distinction
needs to be made: Birney is totally lacking in any sense of Christian
consolation. Above all, his stance is more than just another variation on
the Canadian within a garrison looking out into the uncertainties beyond
civilized boundaries. Birney portrays a contemporary human figure,
aware of the brutalities both outside and within the self, steadfastly
contemplating the not-I. There is always an existential loneliness about
the meditating persona of his finest poems.

The Anglo-Saxon wanderer blends with surprising ease into the sar-
donic, twentieth-century traveller. Clashes between cultural attitudes
('Sinaloa', 'A Walk in Kyoto') give infinite scope to his sense of irony (Birney wrote his doctoral dissertation on 'Chaucer's Irony'), and some of his
best poems derive their strength from a creative balancing of contradictory principles or incompatible responses or conflicting life views. But Birney's tourist persona, about which so much has been written, also needs
qualification. Sometimes, as in the splendid 'Twenty-third Flight' about a
trip to Honolulu ('Yea though I walk through the valley of Immigration / I
fear no evil'), Birney plays the part – albeit with a distancing irony that the
incongruous echoes from the psalm indicate – of the conventional sight-
seer. More often, however, he is as much an observer of tourists as of
foreign lands and customs, establishing an important (characteristically
Canadian?) halfway point between subject seeing and object seen.

He is also an observer of himself. Two of the tourist poems are the-
matically significant in a way that illuminates some of Birney's basic
poetic principles. 'Bangkok Boy', portraying a Thai urchin

> with all
> small
> boys'
> joy
> dancing under the sun

celebrates a momentary unconscious freedom soon to be checked by growth and enforced entry into the constricting adult world. In 'The Bear on the Delhi Road' a shackled bear is being trained by his captors to work as a performer 'in the tranced dancing of men.' Both poems combine the particular and the universal, and contain many implicit meanings. One of these involves the nature of freedom, and it is not illegitimate, I think, to see in them reflections of Birney's attitude to the art of poetry. He envies the freedom of the Thai boy, though he knows its limitations and the hard reality that will soon impinge upon it; he laments the taming of the once-free bear, but knows that art, whether dancing or poetry, demands discipline and intense application.

Birney's travel poetry is generally oral poetry. He forces us to hear the local accents, which are not only part of the sense of difference but often intrinsic to the point of the poem, since unfamiliar attitudes are best caught in unfamiliar phrasing. The contrast between particular dialects (whether Mexican, Caribbean, Australian, American, or Torontonian) and 'standard English' is part of the effect – and (let it not be forgotten) part of the fun. Having learned his craft from the predominantly oral poetry of Old and Middle English, Birney has always laid great emphasis on sound and rhythm. This can occasionally lead him into excess (one wonders if some of his extreme phonetics are worth the trouble of deciphering), but it invigorates his verse with the genuine accents of human speech. It allows him an extraordinary variety from the coarsely strident ('Strine [Australian] Authors Meet') to the delicately modulated (as in some of his accomplished lyric poetry, including the tender love poems of his later years). Throughout his career Birney made poems out of all aspects of his life, and although all sides of the man do not produce poetry of equal quality, his range is nevertheless astonishing. His poetry draws from all the choices that modernism made possible, and creates its own personal synthesis. Behind all the personae, all the linguistic and topographical high jinks, we encounter a dedicated and serious artist who reflects with remarkable cogency what it felt like to be a sensitive and thinking Canadian in the absurd, bewildering, but fascinating world of the mid-twentieth century.

Chapter 5

The Mythic Versus the Human

A recurring pattern of development in Canadian poetry can now be recognized. It proceeds through a series of creative clashes between extremes identified in various phases as British versus North American, cosmopolitan versus native, fine versus crude, and genteel versus vulgar or at least vigorous. In the 1940s this tendency is conveniently illustrated by the appearance of two 'little' but influential magazines in Montréal. *Preview,* led by the English immigrant Patrick Anderson, was decidedly cosmopolitan in its allegiances, though deriving most of its poetic and political attitudes from the Auden group of the 1930s, while *First Statement,* founded by John Sutherland, conspicuously flaunted native energy and originality. The lines were not, of course, tightly drawn. Klein, as we have seen, contributed to both magazines, and Louis Dudek, though formally associated with *First Statement,* steadfastly attempted to find a golden mean between the two basic positions. The title of this chapter refers to a new if related development that began to make itself felt in the 1950s with the appearance of a group of poets who believed that they could achieve universality through conscious employment of myth and archetype as the structural foundation, and even the prime subject matter, of their poetry. Since most available myths were imported from elsewhere (Douglas LePan, in the title of a well-known poem of the 1940s, described Canada as 'a country without a mythology'), the mythopoeic poets generally, though by no means exclusively, adhered to 'cosmopolitan' traditions. They were continually challenged by writers who stressed the individualistic and the vital.

In the 1940s, Dudek and Raymond Souster performed a similar function to that provided by Smith and Scott twenty years before. They were the active champions of a contemporary Canadian poetry, providing outlets for new writers by initiating little magazines, founding small presses, compiling anthologies, and generally agitating for a poetry that came to grips with twentieth-century realities. This is not to say that they agreed with Smith and Scott; on the contrary, they saw the early Canadian modernists as too European (which generally meant British) in their allegiances, and felt the need to express a distinctive North American consciousness. Although in practice this often meant the adoption of models already developed in the United States (Souster in particular found himself attracted to the work of William Carlos Williams, Kenneth Fearing, Charles Olson, Robert Creeley, and Cid Corman), Dudek championed what he called 'truly Canadian and realistic modern poetry' whose language re-created 'Canadian voice and rhythm' rather than 'English metre' (*Selected Essays* 102). The old pendulum continued to swing.

As we look back from his *Collected Poetry* (1971) to his participation in *First Statement*, we note the incongruity of Dudek's presence alongside Souster and Irving Layton. Dudek's flirting with the radical and rebellious proved to be a temporary phase. His increasing commitment to a poetry of reasoned argument and epigrammatic meditation led him further and further from Williams's well-known slogan 'No ideas but in things', and he parted company with Layton as he watched, during the 1960s and 1970s, the forces for revolutionary energy decline into what he later condemned as a new barbarism. 'Order' and 'barbarism' are, indeed, key words in his work. Poetry for Dudek was an assertion of the possibility of order, of civilization in its true sense, against the threat of barbarism and chaos, whether manifest in egalitarian political theory, the strident vulgarities of advertising, or the crudity of capitalist-oriented materialism. In an age that had gone whoring after false freedoms and turned its back on rationalism and traditional values, he was an advocate of 'Mind, the great orchestrator of meaning, / lord of all things that are' (*Atlantis*, III, 1).

Within the context of Canadian poetry, Dudek is unusual in that his best early work is to be found in his long poems, *Europe* (1954), *En México* (1958), and *Atlantis* (1967). *Europe* is of special interest since its subject matter both initiates and depends upon a rethinking of the whole question of cultural tradition. It is as if Dudek consciously reverses the pattern of westward movement, and returns to examine at first hand the continent that saw the birth of modern civilization. In so doing he is following the modernist examples of Pound and Eliot, though Dudek's visit is temporary – he goes openly and deliberately as a tourist. He visits

England (which gave him his language), France (the land of love, reason, and political revolution), and the southern Mediterranean (especially the Classical ruins of Rome and Greece). The sequence is made up of ninety-nine individual sections that record his impressions, thoughts, conclusions. The tone is flexible; he is open to surprises, chance encounters, forced readjustments, though one senses that he approaches each country with questions to be posed, preconceptions to be tested. Although he is a confessed tourist, it is primarily Dudek's mind that travels.

The Europe Dudek finds is still showing the scars of the Second World War. The older ruins tell of ancient empires fallen, the new ones of empires in the process of falling because they have failed to learn the lessons of the past. Here as so often in his work, whether verse or prose, we see in Dudek a civilized man brooding stoically over clear signs of cultural decay. The climax of the book appears as a half sombre, half bracing realization:

It seems that we have come all this distance
to discover the virtues of America (the continent, Canada
being a good part of it).

(Section 84)

Though the point is made quietly, without fuss, it carries considerable force, and thus demonstrates the importance of Dudek's stylistic control. Despite early indications of poetic reference and allusion (the opening poem recalls Homer's *Odyssey* and Pound's first canto), the tone becomes increasingly individual, meditative, discursive. As *Europe* develops, Dudek's diction steadfastly avoids the 'poetic' and his rhythms vary with the nature of the subject and the mood of the observer:

Let your body
move with the rhythm of the ocean,
you can learn to suffer
recorded cacophony, conversation, or cards
clogging the belly,
if you yield to her magnificent surges ...

(Section 18)

The relation of form to content is obvious (perhaps a little too obvious) here, but it soon develops into more direct and abstract meditation:

> As for democracy, it is not just the triumph
>   of superior numbers,
> but that everyone, continually,
> should think and speak the truth.
>
> (Section 83; rev. ed.)

The plainness, the deceptive casualness, is characteristic. This is a voice we learn to trust; even when it seems prosaic, we want to read on.

The later poems move resolutely towards the discursive and the conceptual; we hear the poet in the actual process of thinking. *En México* records a journey with a very different destination, the threatening but exciting vigour of the jungle. He discovers

> the real conditions
> of living, which are universal carnage
> in a jungle of fertility.
>
> (Section 2)

He learns 'the necessary magnificence of *all* reality' (Section 3, my italics). The poetry, despite its abstractions, has become more personal, less rhetorical in tone. We can understand why Dudek was later to define a poem (within a poem) as 'a man talking to himself' (*Continuation 1*, 25). Moreover, the experience of Mexico seems to require him to return to Europe with new eyes and in search of other values. *Atlantis* follows a similar route to *Europe* but in reverse order, and Dudek is now looking for different things. The cultivated (dead) is set against the vulgar (living), but stress is laid firmly upon the latter. Dudek has himself acknowledged that *Europe* looked towards the past whereas *Atlantis* 'is a voyage in search of the present – of reality' (qtd. in Davey and Nichol 54). This reality manifests itself throughout the poem:

> Looking at the cold sculptures
>   in the very cold museum

I saw a work of art walking about.

Her hair was brown and tumbling...

(I, 1)

Atlantis, the imaginary land beneath the ocean, becomes a symbol (the most 'poetic' conception in the poem) of the bedrock reality that all must accept – 'the grey indifference where nothing stands, where only the sea moves, / that is itself nothing, and everything' (Epilogue). The drab eloquence of the verse, containing both splendour and banality, is the perfect embodiment of Dudek's completed journey.

In terms of technique, his later poetry developed even further. *Continuation 1* (1981) is made up of a series of linked epigrams, though the links are not always obvious. 'If it has any order', Dudek wrote in a prefatory note, 'it is an order in the nature of the mind itself'; in other words, his thoughts are believed to form a unity *because* they are all his thoughts. The method obviously has its dangers – the diary form is carried to its limits, and perhaps beyond – but it is consistent with the major preoccupations of his verse. The emphasis on mind, order, reason, and consciousness is paramount. His poetry is always about something, and if it is abstract it is imbued with the 'abstract passion' that he has praised in F. R. Scott (qtd. in Davey and Nichol 297). It exists between the two poles of civilization and the jungle, and its humanism is argued, not assumed. 'There is such a thing as being over-civilized', he admits in *Europe* (Section 36). 'Do the arts matter?' (*En México* Section 1) is a perpetual question, and the affirmative answer is never offered thoughtlessly or glibly. All the more valuable, then, is his firm defence of a discriminated tradition from the past as a model for possible regeneration in a beleaguered present.

Raymond Souster is a prolific writer of short poems, and this constitutes the most obvious difference between his work and Dudek's. Only seldom will a Souster poem stretch over more than one page. The cumulative development of a position is not his *forte;* most of his poems represent brief notations of experience – thoughts, feelings, images occurring naturally in the course of an average day. His *Collected Poems* are intended to preserve only the verse that Souster wishes to retain in print; even so, the first four volumes contain well over a thousand poems.

As might be expected, then, he is a poet for all occasions, though two of his best-known (because most anthologized) poems, 'The Hunter' and 'Flight of the Roller-Coaster', are in fact untypical of his work, the former on account of its rural setting, the latter because of its imaginative fantasy that transcends Souster's habitual realism. He is quintessentially a city poet, and more specifically a poet of Toronto –

> Strange city,
> cold, hateful city,
> that I still celebrate and love.
>
> ('The City Called a Queen')

His subject matter reflects the experience of the average (now urban) man and woman, and he is especially remarkable for presenting with unusual vividness the drab world of monotonous routines and life patterns, material rarely mentioned in 'traditional' verse:

> the years
> of street gangs, corner pool-halls heavy
> with smoke and bravado, dance-hall Saturday nights,
> bottles bulging in suit-coats, girls ready for sex
> in the borrowed car.
>
> ('Court of General Sessions')

He makes poems about a local baseball game, derelicts and prostitutes, a caterpillar in a suburban garden, young love or lust at street corners.

But Souster is important not merely because he revealed new subjects for Canadian poetry but because he encouraged flexibility in form and language. He is suspicious of conventional poetic attitudes, and demonstrates the point, appropriately through levels of language, in the following lines from an early poem:

> Rain on the streets: go ahead, make your little poem
> about wet boughs and the silver sandals
> of the rain; it's still one hell of a night.
>
> ('Night Poem')

Stylistically, Souster maintains the colloquial casualness of the last clause throughout his poetry. He was a pioneer in the introduction into Canadian verse of relaxed language and patterns of speech:

> I want to put it down
> about the animal
> that burrowed its way
> up under my front porch,
>
> but there's not that much
> to say.

('I Want to Put It Down')

The effect lies in the apt combination of simple subject matter and vernacular tone. The stress falls not so much upon the animal as upon the speaker's attitude and stance. Within the development of Canadian poetic techniques, we can recognize Souster as paving the way for the chirpy, no-nonsense style of Purdy.

At their best, Souster's poems perfectly sum up experiences and reactions that the reader may have shared but never articulated; at their worst they can be sentimental, banal, falsely strident, but never pretentious or verbose. Souster's powers of self-criticism are curiously limited. Too often the genuineness of a sentiment blinds him to the inadequacy of its expression, and the *Collected Poems* would be considerably improved by rigorous pruning. In general, he is better when offering images rather than assertions, and far better displaying compassion than expressing either anger or contempt. His strength lies in immediacy, but this is sometimes bought at the price of subtlety. There has been comparatively little development in his poetry; his subjects and general attitudes have remained much the same. Above all, he has never evolved anything approaching a philosophy of life. Where Dudek moved towards general statement and broader understanding – his recurring voyage-metaphor itself is an emblem of his mental journey – Souster has put his faith in the here and now, in the world of things. Both are centrally concerned with the human and the humane, but Dudek ponders over life while Souster portrays it. Dudek is a humanistic intellectual, Souster a man – and poet – of the people.

In addition to Dudek and Souster – and Layton (whom I shall discuss later) – this period saw the emergence of a number of accomplished, highly intelligent and articulate poets who, without producing work that radically altered the map of the country's literature, contributed impressively to the quantity and quality of 'modernist' Canadian poetry. Most of these writers emphasized human responses in an age of political trauma (the Second World War, the beginning of the Atomic Age), and were faithful to traditional humanistic values. Their work stressed continuity rather than startling originality, and although some of them have been criticized for cultural timidity and cosmopolitan aloofness, their emphasis on poetic craft and texture, stylistic polish, and intellectual rigour was both valuable and influential. They built, one might say, on the foundations that Smith had laid.

It is hardly surprising, then, that Smith wrote one of the earliest and most satisfying discussions of the poetry of P. K. Page (*Towards a View* 146–55). Page was a member of the *Preview* group, and her initial poetic aim seems to have been to envelop the lives and work of ordinary people in a golden net of verse. The much-anthologized 'Stenographers' is one example among many. Similarly, the main figure in 'The Landlady', spying on her tenants,

> Wonders when they are quiet, jumps when they move,
> dreams that they dope or drink, trembles to know
> the traffic of their brains, jaywalks their street
> in clumsy shoes.

The expansion of the 'traffic' metaphor through 'jaywalks' and 'street' to 'shoes' is typical. Here and elsewhere (in 'T-Bar', for example) we are reminded of the heightened observation and verbal dexterity of Klein, about whom Page has written sympathetically. Her verse is intellectually exhilarating to read, though the technical brilliance can separate the reader from the subject. We are sometimes dazzled by the rhetoric and so miss the meaning.

A highly self-conscious poet, Page is acutely aware of this tendency. In 'Leviathan in a Pool' she begins with a flood of metaphor and allusion, then comments: 'So much for linear description / phrases in place of whale.' Her later poetry, however, has tended to move away from social and political concerns (the legacy of Auden's thirties) to concentrate on the creative powers of the mind as manifest in significant dreams and mystical experience. 'The greatest poetry', she has said in an interview, 'is the poetry of the higher imagination' (Pearce 153). Page herself aims high, and in this rarefied atmosphere her close-packed figurative style is decidedly more appropriate. The visionary implications inherent in the exquisite and surprisingly early 'Stories of Snow' are developed in such poems as 'Images of Angels', 'Arras', and 'Cry Ararat!' As before, these poems are lacquered with image and metaphor, but this style assists in developing 'the eye of the mind' ('A Backwards Journey') so that it can achieve, in one of Page's typical phrases, 'the focus of the total I' ('Cry Ararat!'). The I/eye pun is central to Page. She aims, with Blake, to look not with but through the eye, and she values art not only for itself but for its capacity to reach towards a cosmic unity. As she writes in 'For Mstislav Rostropovich with Love',

> Perfection in an art
> can heal an open wound,
> a broken heart
> or fuse fragmented man.

Douglas LePan resembles Page in his propensity for verbal richness, metaphorical abundance, elaborate diction, and sonorous rhythms; but he put these effects to very different purpose. Page is more obviously cosmopolitan. Although poems occasionally reflect her travels with her diplomat husband to Australia, Brazil, and Mexico, her work generally transcends locality. Only a few references suggest Canada. But LePan has a number of poems in *The Wounded Prince* (1948) and *Something Still to Find* (1982) in which the condition of Canada is central, while the Second World War poems in *The Net and the Sword* (1953), set for the most part in Italy, depend for their effect on a Canadian, non-European speaker.

In all three volumes, a subtle tension is created between subject matter and the style that envelops it. The Canadian speakers in *The Wounded Prince* reproduce the cadences of the English tradition, and this emphasizes the stark challenge of the country they confront. The stranger in 'A Country without a Mythology' encounters 'this savage people' and the threatening final image is that of a 'lust-red manitou'. The 'curious country' of 'Canoe-Trip' is initially seen in terms of Old-World heraldry ('the lions of gold and gules'), but 'Let whoever comes to tame this land, beware!' The warning applies, one assumes, as much to eloquent poets as to adventurous prospectors. More disturbingly, in 'Coureurs de Bois' the 'desperate wilderness' is found to be eternal (compare 'A Rough Sweet Land' later in which 'Two hundred years are nothing, nothing'); the 'perilous' voyage 'into the dark interior', though less threatening than that in Conrad's *Heart of Darkness,* is only superficially geographical. In such circumstances, language both controls and consoles.

In *The Net and the Sword* the ornate vocabulary at first seems incongruous when applied to the squalor and sordidness of war:

> O much traduced
> And tarnished flesh, when guns and hungers peal,
> Abandoned here beneath the blow of history.
>
> ('Elegy in the Romagna')

Once again, however, the speaker needs the continuities of language and ordered thought to keep sane in a world of chaos. The articulation is therapeutic. References to earlier wars, and the realization that from a historical perspective the 'ravishing tread that hunts for loot' can be 'Visigoth or Canadian' ('Tuscan Villa'), similarly establish continuity and so impose sense on the senseless. For LePan 'Intelligence-and-Power, the lost archangel' ('Angels and Artificers') is all-important. Although we are continually reminded, through carefully placed image and allusion, that he is Canadian in inspiration and attitude, as sensitive meditating poet he becomes representative of all thinking men. Within his verse human dignity is asserted and upheld.

Both Ralph Gustafson and Margaret Avison belong to the generation of writers already discussed, but, although they began writing in the 1930s, they did not achieve prominence until much later. Both are known as rewarding but difficult poets, and both derive this reputation, at least in part, from their common interest in Gerard Manley Hopkins. (One of Gustafson's volumes is entitled *Sift in an Hourglass.*) For both, the world is charged with the grandeur of God, though in Gustafson's case this awareness was accompanied by no explicit religious belief. He speaks at

one point of his 'faith / in nothing and poems' ('The Churches at Kiev').
Like Hopkins, he had to write the influence of the major Romantics out
of his system, and he gradually evolved his own resonant and elliptical
style that is rendered complex by the wide range of his knowledge and
interests. Gustafson was, in many respects, the well-rounded Renaissance
man, a learned poet – seemingly interested in everything – who wrote
with impressive authority about the natural world, painting, architecture,
literature, music, and a poetically transformed science. As he remarks in
'The Sun in the Garden', 'I sit in the sun / And think of astrophysics'. He
responds keenly to 'All That Is in the World' (to quote a poem title), and it
is always within matter and the senses that he finds the principle he calls
God.

His mature work (only manifesting itself in 1960 with the publication of *Rivers among Rocks* and *Rocky Mountain Poems*) may be divided
into three main parts: close-packed, almost 'metaphysical' but often enigmatic lyrics and meditations; poem series recording particular linked
experiences (*Rocky Mountain Poems; Soviet Poems,* 1978); and more
direct, explicit poems based on national and political events (*Themes and
Variations for Sounding Brass,* 1972). His style is marked by a kind of colloquial intellectualism: the references are erudite, but the tone communicates directness and intimacy. It is the obscurity of his syntax that causes
difficulties – at times he seems not so much to dominate language as to
shatter it. Too often one feels that he jumps bewilderingly from private
response to private response, merely listing allusions; not enough is done
poetically with the references and paradoxes paraded before us. This is
less evident in poems about the natural world, whether romantic scenery
or the quiet ordinariness of his garden, and the tension between these
generally New-World subjects and the high art and traditions of the Old
World creates that sensuous piquancy in his poetry comparable to an
acquired taste in wine. Above all, he is intensely alive to the extraordinary
contrasts in the world he celebrates:

> My soul is utterly taken by the man
> Selling Coke from a red refrigerator
> On the roof of Milan Cathedral.
>
>   ('On the Top of Milan Cathedral'.)

All that is in the world, indeed.

Margaret Avison's first three published volumes record three distinct stages in her development as human being and as poet. *Winter Sun* (1960) is a quest for meaning in a dark, wintry world, and ends on the brink of illumination but without achieving it and without quite believing in its possibility. *The Dumbfounding* (1966), published after her conversion to a Christianity emphasizing work and example rather than meditation and dogma, is a presentation of inexplicable 'grace' in which the poet is paradoxically dumbfounded into eloquent praise. *Sunblue* (1978) celebrates moments of ordinary perception now apparelled in celestial light. One thinks, however, of Hopkins rather than Wordsworth, not only because of the violent intensity of her newly acquired faith, but because of the wrenched syntax and contorted language that uses unexpected juxtapositions to achieve powerful but unusual verbal effects. Many of the short 'sketch' poems in *Sunblue*, for example, offer Hopkinsian inscapes, concentrated essences of experience, as here:

> Storm-heaped west, wash-soaked with
> dayspill. Light's combers
> broken, suds-streaming
> > darkwards and stormwards.
>
> > > ('The Seven Birds')

The difficulty of her poetry stems from her insistence that the reader's imagination, the 'optic heart' as she calls it in 'Snow', should participate actively in the poetic experience. She makes no concessions, and this sometimes results in an apparent formlessness – as if the reader is expected to supply the structure as well as an illuminating comprehension. A related difficulty for the critic is the temptation to expound, to paraphrase, to lose the poetry in a search for meaning. The poems in *Winter Sun* are especially challenging, and Avison has herself acknowledged the excessive obscurity of her early verse. By the same token, some of the poems in *Sunblue* seem too directly assertive, too content to end up on a Christian allusion which the unconvinced may see as no more than a tag. Some of her best work appears in *The Dumbfounding* in poems like 'The Word', the title poem, and 'Searching and Sounding', where Christian illumination is conveyed with a superb control of rhythm and technical effect (including deeply serious puns). Elsewhere her irregular lines and apparently rambling structures seem strange within the context of Canadian traditionalism. Many of her earlier poems, indeed, first appeared in American magazines, and her work fits well into the 'projectivist' movement that linked such poets as Olson, Creeley, and Corman. But perhaps Avison is never more Canadian than in her ability to combine this spare American neo-modernism with Hopkinsian exuberance.

The poets I have just discussed stressed the whole range and complexity of human learning, endeavour, and achievement. Others, at the same time, were more interested in the ordinary patterns and processes of living, of the subjects available in their own (Canadian) backyards. John Glassco, best known for his prose confessions *Memoirs of Montparnasse,* was especially aware, within his own experience, of the split between international and local. Many of his poems ('The Cardinal's Dog (*Musée d'Autun*)', 'Utrillo's World') treat subjects that might have inspired Gustafson to flights of puzzling brilliance, though Glassco writes of them coolly, directly, with dry irony. But a considerable section of his *Selected Poems* is devoted to quiet, polished verse meditations on the Québec farming country in which he lived much of his life. In such poetry we hear the thoughtful, resigned, restrained rhythms of a man who never raises his voice, who says what he means with verbal skill but without grand effects.

The countryside about which he writes is beautiful but depressed, even desolate; the farm buildings are often in ruins. But Glassco, sensitive to 'time's insulting accidents', and possessed of 'a heart / That loves the fading attitude', responds to 'the native angles of decay / In shed and barn' ('Deserted Buildings under Shefford Mountain'). He displays an affection, even while he criticizes, for 'the inane, imagined verities / In the soil, the dung, the teats' ('Gentleman's Farm'). 'Luce's Notch' with its deliberately slack iambic pentameter (occasionally Frost-like but for a different purpose) catches the acute but curiously deadened sensibility of the inner man. These poems impress cumulatively as a remarkable sequence – more successful, in my opinion, than his uneven and prosaic *Montreal* (1973). Although in a minor key, this is the controlled voice of a master.

Miriam Waddington published her early poetry in both *Preview* and

First Statement, though her prime allegiances were with the latter. Her poems range from those arising out of her experience as a social worker and those expressing a personal but elusive lyricism. She published volumes quietly but steadily throughout her life, and gradually evolved a characteristic manner. She once asserted in an interview: 'My language has always been undated, because I have always liked and tried to use colloquial, conversational language' (Pearce 178). This is true so far as her vocabulary is concerned, but it took her a long time to develop a colloquial, relaxed rhythm. Her early poems, though accomplished, often seemed to lack a clear sense of direction. She achieved a stylistic breakthrough with *The Glass Trumpet* (1966), where her lines became conspicuously, almost obsessively short:

> Of course he knows
> people still live
> in the ruins
> right here in
> this lovely city
> right here behind
> the old hospital ...
>
> ('Summer Letters')

In the same volume she finds her best subject – 'Things of the World', which become 'the good things of the world' in the poem of that name.

She moved, then, from formality to colloquial ease. Consequently her poetry became localized – she can now sing 'A Song of North York between Sheppard and Finch'. Although her love poems can sometimes become searingly eloquent, one does not expect her to produce hauntingly memorable lines in the manner of Layton. But there is a limpid quality to her verse that proves especially appealing. Her work has been underrated because it looks both easier and simpler than it is. Her ability to write intimately without becoming excessively private was the result of a long and arduous apprenticeship.

The poetry of George Johnston is unusual in its humour (comic poetry is surprisingly rare in Canada), its presentation of middle-class domesticity (which is lovingly as well as ironically presented), and, at least in his early verse, in its preference for suburban settings. It is especially remarkable for its poise. Johnston could move quickly and skillfully from humour to pathos and back again, and was particularly adept in inserting a chilling note into his superficially light verse. Thus 'An Affluent Guest' begins in modern suburbia with a 'thawed-out meal' but ends with a consideration of 'God's multiplying damned'. In 'War on the Periphery' the gentle narrator peacefully leading his 'small suburban life' acknowledges sadly that his comfort depends upon but is also threatened by 'The violent, obedient ones / Guarding my family with guns'. Johnston invariably made poetry out of what he saw around him – often quite literally, as in this rural example:

> The green we see
>   from our kitchen:
> Fred's oatfield,
>   Aging now, turning bronze.
>
> ('Thrash')

But his simplicity, like Waddington's, is deceptive; technically, this is evident in his control of traditional and regular rhyming stanzas, which never descend into doggerel unless the poet wants a jingling effect.

His later poetry is equally domestic but more personal and intimate ('A Visit', 'Company of the Dead', 'Back to the Ironbound Shore'). Here he also shows himself as an excellent 'occasional' poet, as in his tonally assured 'Convocation Address' in verse, and in the various poems to friends in *Taking a Grip*. This apparent casualness may place him on the periphery of modern verse movements, but he found a neglected plot of poetic ground and proceeded to cultivate it to perfection. The later verse, in particular, takes on a stylistic subtlety derived from his experience as a translator from the Icelandic. Here direct rhyme is likely to be replaced by alliteration, accentual beats, half-rhymes, and assonantal rhyme. His poetry gains authority from the generally inconspicuous rigour of his craft. For all his stress on ordinariness, he was one of the most technically sophisticated of modern Canadian poets.

'The mythopoeic poets', like most labels, doubtless suggests a more cohesive group than ever actually existed. Nevertheless, it roughly categorizes a poetic movement centred in Toronto during the 1950s and notable for the work of James Reaney, Jay Macpherson, and others united by an interest in the literary theorizing of Northrop Frye. Frye himself has rightly protested that he was not, as has sometimes been implied, a critic-guru dictating a mythic approach to the writing of verse: 'There is no Frye school of mythopoeic poetry; criticism and poetry cannot possibly be related in that way' (*Divisions* 23). His influence was, however, strong: Macpherson's *The Boatman* is dedicated to the Fryes, while in his editorial to the first issue of *Alphabet*, a magazine devoted to 'the iconography of the imagination' which he founded in 1960 and which proved an important outlet for poets with similar interests, Reaney looks back nostalgically to 'the months when young men and women sat up all night reading [Frye's] *Fearful Symmetry* which had just come out'. To these poets Frye's beliefs concerning the mythic structure of the imagination, a coherent pattern of imagery which exists in the universe and is available – indeed, integral – to art, served as a creative release. Moreover, as his editor Germaine Warkentin has noted, Reaney is 'a truly mythopoeic poet' since his poems 'do not record the world for us, they re-make the world on an entirely visionary model' (*Selected Shorter Poems*, 1975, 7).

The group is sometimes criticized for its academicism, and it is true that many of its members were also scholars with university appointments who bring a background of learning to their own verse. Macpherson wrote her master's thesis on Milton's pastoral and published a textbook on Classical mythology; Reaney's doctoral dissertation was on Spenser and Yeats. But these traditional poets, together with Blake and the Bible as filtered through Frye's writings, offered a poetic structure that reflected universal patterns of imagery and modes of symbolic thought. Frye himself interpreted this interest on the part of the young poets of the 1950s as essentially progressive, as 'the growth of an unforced and relaxed sense of cultural tradition' (*Divisions* 23), and certainly the influence of these writers is in turn reflected in the work of Gwendolyn MacEwen (see Volume Two) and the young Margaret Atwood.

Reaney dominated this group by virtue of his varied talents and irrepressible energy. *The Red Heart*, his first volume of verse, appeared as early as 1948, and most of these poems were written before Frye could have had any substantial influence upon him. Like nothing else in earlier Canadian literature, the book is clearly the product of a precocious, gifted, and decidedly eccentric talent. Far from being universally archetypal, it is fiercely regional in its reference and force. All the poems of this period (there are others collected in the 1972 *Poems*) seem to be narrated by a lonely southern Ontario farm boy possessing a child's play-box and a Gothic temperament. He cherishes the myths he derives from books (especially the Bible) and tries to reconcile them with the strange world that exists about him. The poems are by turns macabre, fanciful, healthily and unhealthily imaginative, naive, shrewd, and piercingly sensitive. Atwood's phrase 'unprecedented weirdness' (*Second Words* 151) sums them up as well as any. This poetry shows extraordinary promise but lacks a sense of total achievement. Some of the imagery is dazzlingly evocative – 'Apples fell like desultory tennis' ('The Birth of Venus'), 'geese white as pillows' ('The Upper Canadian'). Technically the lines are often brilliant, yet sometimes they falter or refuse to flow, and the result is rhythmic uncertainty. The boy's viewpoint itself can be magnificently effective – it represents a triumph of dreaming backwards (to borrow from Eli Mandel borrowing from Yeats) – but it is also a limitation: the sublimely innocent childlike can easily degenerate into the embarrassingly self-indulgent childish.

A Suit of Nettles, which followed in 1958, is the most vulnerable of Reaney's books to the charge of being excessively academic. It is based structurally, and often stylistically, on Spenser's *Shepheardes Calendar*. Reaney attempts to localize (and so 'Canadianize') the external conventions of pastoral by setting this long poem in an Ontario farmyard (the chief characters are Ontario geese). The traditional frame (twelve sections, one for each month of the season cycle) allows for all kinds of subjects – romance, education, history, philosophy, even birth control – and the poem is in many respects a bizarre, even knockabout intellectual romp. But Reaney never quite succeeds in reconciling his erudite and distant source with his immediate and local purpose, and the verse fluctuates between lively experimentation and (too often) a tedious and heavy-footed form of pastiche. Reaney's tendency towards whimsical self-indulgence, even to the point of self-parody, is never more evident than here.

By contrast, *Twelve Letters to a Small Town* (1962) represents his best poetic work. The loving focus on Stratford, Ontario, re-creates the town in such a way that nostalgia and history are humanly balanced, and the chapbook anticipates that exploration of a local past that has exercised many Canadian poets in subsequent decades. Moreover, the opening poem, 'To the Avon River above Stratford, Canada', is quite simply Reaney's masterpiece, where all his strengths are manifest and none of his weaknesses. The language and tone are subtly controlled and totally at one with the content:

> before
> I drank coffee or tea
> I drank you
> with my cupped hands
> And you did not taste English to me.

Reaney establishes perfectly a unique but representative Canadian sense of difference, achieved without nationalistic blather, but firmly and maturely independent in its insistence on defining and articulating its own place. The whole book moves towards the same ideal, though it never quite attains the perfection of this opening poem. Unfortunately, *The Dance of Death at London, Ontario* (1963) is a sad plunge from the standard of its predecessor, and since then Reaney has turned his main attention to drama. A highly talented though quirky poet, he has not achieved what he ought to have achieved because he has never disciplined his wayward poetic intelligence, but he remains, especially in Ontario, an engaging if often infuriating presence.

In Jay Macpherson's work the pattern of myth is seen in its purest form. Indeed, *The Boatman* (1957) has been called 'the most intricately unified book in Canadian poetry' (Munro Beattie, LHC II, 300). She creates a timelessness and placelessness – there is no 'Canadian content' unless we count the title of 'True North'; this poetry exists completely in the here and now of art. Traditional symbols (ark, labyrinth, garden, island) and traditional figures (Adam and Eve, pastoral shepherds, mermaid, sibyl) are explored and revivified. Technique is everything, and Macpherson's technique is impeccable. She is highly eclectic and allusive, expecting her readers to pick up references to the main monuments of Western literature, but these are offered with a studied casualness. Hers is essentially a minimal art (only the opening poem extends beyond a single page). She can sum up the whole of Book IX of *Paradise Lost* in the first five words of 'Eve in Reflection', 'Painful and brief the act', and the pun in the title (fallen Eve is watching and thinking about the reflection in water of her unfallen state) is typical. While verbally fastidious, Macpherson can spice her chastely lucid diction with dashes of the slangily colloquial. Similarly, the solemn is frequently punctuated by the playful, both in individual poems ('Ordinary People in the Last Days') and in the way one poem is played off against another. The most perfectly constructed ark in *The Boatman* (which contains a sequence of eight ark poems) is the volume itself.

In *Welcoming Disaster* (1974) an overall unity is again prominent, though the playful is interspersed with the solemn rather than vice versa. Nevertheless, the book offers an almost Jungian archetypal pattern of descent and rebirth in a surprisingly whimsical context where the main characters are female guide and silent teddy-bear (perhaps the ambiguous influence of Reaney). This is a highly self-conscious book, insisting on especially intricate metrical forms at a time when vers libre seemed to have carried all before it, and the conspicuous Sapphics, though skillfully managed, give the impression of existing as a self-imposed exercise. More personal than *The Boatman*, *Welcoming Disaster* seems at the same time more remote. Macpherson is, it must be conceded, a minor poet, but, having accepted her limitations, she achieves formal and stylistic perfection within her own boundaries. Perhaps ultimately a poet's poet, she can delight, with wit, polish, and profundity, anyone capable of appreciating the beauty of sheer artifice.

But 'let us compare mythologies'. Leonard Cohen's evocative first title reminds us that myth was not the exclusive preserve of the Toronto poets of the period, and that it could be used poetically for very different effects. 'Beside the Shepherd', the last poem in *Let Us Compare Mythologies* (1956), may begin like a poem by Macpherson, while 'A Kite Is a Victim', the opening poem in *The Spice-Box of Earth* (1961), may reveal something of the cogent naivety of Reaney, but both display the unmistakable impress of Cohen's early style. In his first book he sets his own Jewish cultural tradition against a whole range of others, but particularly the Christian (as in 'For Wilf and His House') and the Greek (as in 'The Song of the Hellenist'). In the former, for instance, he explains how

> When young the Christians told me
> how we had pinned Jesus

like a lovely butterfly against the wood,

but by the end of the poem the tone changes to 'how my fathers nailed him / like a bat against a barn'. His poems are often, as here, mythical and personal at the same time. Thus Michael Ondaatje claims that the opening poem in *Let Us Compare Mythologies*, 'Elegy', is about a drowned friend (*Leonard Cohen* 8), but the poem itself suggests that the subject (at least, the main subject) is Orpheus. Like Macpherson's, these poems, despite occasional references to pogroms and modern corporations, seem timeless. Unabashedly literary in allusion, the echoes run the gamut from T. S. Eliot to Dylan Thomas, but they create a resonance that is pure Leonard Cohen. The youthful romantic vagueness of his early poetry can be haunting and, within the limits of its somewhat blurred aestheticism, deeply satisfying.

But Cohen is interested in creating mythologies as well as comparing them. Macpherson, in poems like 'The Fisherman', sometimes constructed new myths out of the individual building blocks of the old. Cohen carries the process further in poems like 'Lovers', 'Letter', and 'Warning', and still further in *The Spice-Box of Earth* ('If It Were Spring', 'The Girl Toy'), though we can see here a significant evolution from self-conscious myth-poetry to a simple lyricism that nevertheless relies on basic mythic structures and allusions. In both books, but especially in the second, in poems like 'Saviours' and 'The Boy's Beauty', we find anticipations of the decadent extremism that is accentuated in his later verse, but *The Spice-Box of Earth* is remarkable for its tender and even traditional lyric qualities, for an elegant rhetoric, and for a curious wistfulness that always seems on the brink of violence and horror.

In a notorious (later suppressed) statement on the cover of the original edition of *Flowers for Hitler* (1964) Cohen claimed that the book moved him 'from the world of the golden-boy poet into the dung pile of the front-line writer'. But in fact this new phase, for all its difference in tone, bears striking resemblances to the old. Specific contemporary references (to Cuba, Eichmann, the tensions of Montréal in the early 1960s) take precedence over mythical ones, but much of the decadent-romantic treatment remains. There is the same directness of eloquent statement linked with a deliberately vague openness of meaning, the same deadpan resonance of language. Images of the Jewish holocaust are still exploited, fierce juxtapositions of the gently idyllic with the violently horrific still occur, and formal ballad-quatrains are to be found in most of the later volumes. What develops is an ambiguous posturing that blurs the line between genuine seriousness and mocking parody. 'No instructions come / on how to read this', we are told in 'We Call It Sunlight' (*The Energy of Slaves*, 1972). Cohen creates a situation in which he can smile enigmatically whether he is lionized or denigrated. And in his pop-singer phase he becomes a coarsened parody of his earlier self, the myth-maker self-consciously transformed into a myth.

Like Cohen, most other writers who came within the orbit of the mythopoeic group evolved a kind of poetry that, while indirectly reflecting its mythic origins, does not limit itself to deliberate reinterpretations of mythic patterns and stories. The poetry of Anne Wilkinson, for instance, stands apart from the rest (partly because she was a generation older), but may reasonably be considered within this context. While she revels in sensual experience which leads to a boldness of metaphor suggesting the work of Dylan Thomas, she is highly sensitive to the repeating seasonal patterns of natural processes and the myths to which they give rise. Or, to approach the point from another direction, she employs mythopoeic structures to organize her responses to nature. Alert to 'our myth-told-many-a-bed-time tale' ('Winter Sketch') and 'the myths of my kin' ('Roches Point'), she is nevertheless conscious that her 'lens is grafted from a jungle eye' ('Tigers Know from Birth'), and the title of a late poem, 'Nature Be Damned', is indicative of the pull between natural process and the human myth that attempts to explain and contain it. Some poems, like 'Adam and God' which reverses the story of the seven days of creation by presenting God as created by man and her rewritings of traditional ballads and songs ('After the Ballad "Lord Randall My Son"' or 'Dirge', which reinterprets 'Who Killed Cock Robin?'), proceed in ways that can be labelled mythopoeic; others ('The Up and Down of It', 'Swimming Lesson') create new myths to replace or revivify the old. But most often she clothes the natural world in a splendid patina of resonant language –

> In June and gentle oven
> Summer kingdoms simmer
> As they come

And flower and leaf and love

Release

Their sweetest juice

('In June and Gentle Oven')

– and drops subtle hints that invite associations with traditional patterns and legends, generally Hebrew or Greek. A cunning blend of the communally mythic and the individually human, her poetry succeeds by an imagistic audacity that propels the reader to partake of the poet's vision and assures respect and acceptance by the confidence of its rhetorical control.

The early poetry of Eli Mandel was so preoccupied with Old Testament and Classical legends or allusions that even Frye, reviewing his 'Minotaur Poems', referred to 'his superimposed mythopoeic imagery' (*Bush Garden* 43). But what is noticeable from the perspective of his later work is the emphasis on violence contained within the distancing mythic structure. It seems as if mythopoeic reference, like a mirror against Medusa, protected both reader and poet against direct confrontation with cruelty and horror. In his later verse, however, Mandel spoke out from his own experience – or that of contemporary humanity – responding to the dark world of his own times. One poem, 'On the 25th Anniversary of the Liberation of Auschwitz', typifies his preoccupation. He had become a politically oriented poet ('On the Death of Ho Chi Minh', 'On the Murder of Salvador Allende'); his intellectuality changed from scholarly allusion to cryptic assertion. His poetry was still obsessed with images of death, imprisonment, madness, and he remained a 'difficult' poet since the range of his interests always threatened to lead to an intellectually private verse. But the mythopoeic traces also remained. In *Out of Place* (1977), for example, an imaginative re-creation of his Saskatchewan origins, he appears to offer his own contribution to the poetic-historic documentary (complete with photographs) in which poets such as Al Purdy and Don Gutteridge explore their own 'place'. But the book is structured around a half mythic, half psychological journey and haunted by the figure of the *Doppelgänger*. Mandel avoided the escapism that is a possible fate for the narrower myth-poets, but his later work still bore the impress of his earlier manner. He was, we might say, a Jewish adventurer of the spirit exploring the dark labyrinth of the twentieth century, never quite certain whether his personal threatening Minotaur was an external force or an internal fact.

In the work of D. G. Jones we can trace not only a development from a mythopoeic to a more direct and personal poetry but a parallel shedding of remnants of metrical regularity in favour of a sensitive free verse. The pressure towards mythic allusion seems strong in *Frost on the Sun* (1957); when Jones sees an image of Hermes on Mount Royal and likens Li Po embracing the moon in the Yellow River to Classical Narcissus, he is comparing mythologies. This tendency culminates in the title poem of *Phrases from Orpheus* (1967); nevertheless, even in his early self-conscious verse natural images continually break through the mythological references and the preoccupations with art. Thus 'schoolgirls' in a poem of that title are described as 'Like juncos, or some bird of Klee', and the combinations of natural and artistic is typical. But the more imagistic poems ('Public Figure', 'The Phoebe', 'On the 24th of May', all bird or animal poems) frequently seem more satisfying. Often, indeed ('Little Night Journey' in *The Sun Is Axeman*, 1961, provides an example), one suspects that Jones is trying to rewrite Archibald Lampman for modern taste. And *Under the Thunder the Flowers Light Up the Earth* (1977), his most accomplished volume, contains 'Kate, These Flowers (The Lampman Poems)', which are Jones's renditions of love poems that Lampman himself could never write. In *Under the Thunder* Jones has escaped from the limitations of the mythic, though he retains a preoccupation with art – there are sequences of poems inspired by David Milne and Alex Colville. But these are, of course, Canadian artists. Jones abandons the cosmopolitan mythic for the local and the native; moreover, he treats his subject with a new limidity that can even convey subtle ambivalence through graceful puns. So 'A Garland for Milne' begins: 'He lived in the bush, the wilderness / but he made light of it'. Jones has made a complex poetic journey towards simplicity, and though he sometimes becomes puzzlingly private this later poetry displays the confidence and assurance of artistic maturity.

I have left discussion of Irving Layton to the end of this chapter for two reasons: first, though he began publishing with the *First Statement* group in the early 1940s, he did not become a dominant force until the middle of the next decade; second, his energy and rhetoric are such that they are likely to overwhelm anything that follows. He was clearly the pre-eminent figure during this period; moreover, through his notoriety as a television personality he drew popular attention to artists in general and poets in particular at a time when the arts in Canada were in desperate need of publicity of any kind. For all the opposition he created through his determination to shock the bourgeois and the puritanical, his public demonstration that poets were not to be classed automatically as aesthetic weaklings or irrelevant anomalies was undoubtedly salutary. Much of the upsurge in Canadian poetic activity and achievement from the 1950s onwards came as a result of his often infuriating but always stimulating example. His whole career may be interpreted as an assertion of human vitality over Dudekian intellect, Frye-encouraged myth, or (for Layton worst of all) the general timidity of the cultural mandarins. Layton by no means lacked intellectual depth or eschewed mythic reference, but he insisted that poetry should be an uninhibited product of the whole man.

The first aspect of Layton's poetry that needs to be stressed is its extraordinary range of subject matter, approach, tone, and style. This can be conveniently tested by comparing the tender grace of 'Song for Naomi' with the savage invective of 'Family Portrait'. If we begin by concentrating on his more lyrical poems, we notice at once his wonderful capacity for creating unforgettable lines that haunt the mind. Here are a few examples from his earlier work: 'the immortal claptrap of poetry' ('Seven O'Clock Lecture'); 'Death is a name for beauty not in use' ('Composition in Late Spring'); 'All my ribs most unpaganlike ache / With foolstruck Adam in his first wonder' ('La Minerve'); 'An atheist shivering with blessed ecstasy' ('New Tables'). The first of these extracts is from a poem that has been faulted for its 'flamboyance', its 'embarrassing Romantic clichés' (Mandel, *Irving Layton*, 22; Milton Wilson in Mayne, 78). But of course it is flamboyant, and what Layton has to say would certainly be cliché-ridden if it were more indifferently phrased. His critics have underestimated the magic of words (which, at his best, is Layton's great glory) and the dramatized exasperation which the poem expresses and which is part of its point. After all, it is a 'lecture', a performance, and Layton's performance was an essential ingredient of his verse. In all these instances he took Romantic (surely universal) commonplaces, and made them new. He was big enough not to be afraid of the large gesture.

Layton's poetic method is well illustrated by the following stanza from 'Autumn Lines for My Son':

In death's flaring athanor how beautiful
The trees! Look, the October landscape is
Lovely and dying like a consumptive
Keats – O red-haired runt, I would have poets
Hard as munition-makers, pitiless.

The movement in thought from the colour of the Canadian fall expressed as a metaphor from alchemy to a dying poet and ultimately to a strong Nietzschean assertion is typical of Layton; he works here through poetic logic by which a collision of references sparks off an imaginative chain reaction fusing disparate images into a seemingly inevitable verbal texture. To a considerable extent, of course, this fusion is achieved by the resonance of Layton's rhetoric; like Pratt's, his lines ask to be rolled appreciatively around the tongue. 'Poets', he wrote, 'must insist on the supreme role of the imagination, intellect and passion in the making of poetry ... [and] a quality of workmanship that has all but disappeared from contemporary verse' (*Engagements* 134). This is the traditional stance of the Romantic poet and shows how Layton, for all his blustering contemporaneity, had his roots deep in the literature of the Western tradition of the past two centuries.

But if part of Layton was an unabashedly Romantic poet, another part was Classical in style, reference, and attitude. Throughout his work we find poems with titles like 'Orpheus in Limbo', 'Nausicäa', 'Homage to Lucullus', 'A Roman Jew to Ovid', 'After Theognis'. Often they are written in the poised, conversational style that recalls the Roman satiric poets. Thus 'The Way of the World' begins:

It has taken me long, Lygdamus,
        to learn that humans, barring
a few saints, are degenerate
        or senseless.

Perhaps because of Layton's prominent anti-academic stance, or an assumption that poets should be confined to one pigeonhole, most critics

(Mandel was a notable exception) have tended to overlook, misread, or underestimate this aspect of his poetry, an aspect that becomes more evident in his later verse and blends into his own brand of *saeva indignatio* that owes little to Classical ideals of moderation. Layton himself saw an important phase of his creative life ending in 1958. In the foreword to *A Red Carpet for the Sun* (1959), which collects the best of his early verse and remains a key volume for any serious study of his poetry, he described this period as one of 'testing, confusion, ecstasy'. It was predominantly Romantic in tone, though several of the poems mentioned above are included within it. But later, the balance within the poetry changes. Previously, poems of bitter anguish at man's inhumanity to man provided a sobering undertone to his celebration of 'joyous impermanency' ('At the Barcelona Zoo'); in his later work the dark vision was in the ascendant. It led to poems that are harsh and ugly in sentiment and language, to the satirical squibs that have been the most controversial elements in Layton's always controversial verse.

At this point we encounter head-on one of the perennially contentious issues in the discussion of Canadian literature: the relative claims of vulgarity and gentility, or what has come to be known as the crude/fine distinction. It has been with us ever since Susanna Moodie wrote in *Roughing It in the Bush* of seeing Irish immigrants throw off civilized (European) restraints as they landed on the new continent. With the strange Canadian fondness for establishing polarities, it has developed into a separation of body from mind, an assumption that people upholding traditional standards and values are lacking in passion and vitality. Layton had contributed to this over-simple dichotomy by his recurrent references to 'culture-philistines ... who fear to hear the truth spoken boldly and imaginatively' (Foreword, *Balls for a One-Armed Juggler*, 1964). But Layton himself was a traditionalist in that he upheld the best of the human ideals that have come down to us from the past (especially from his Jewish past) and his already-quoted remark about the combination of 'imagination, intellect and passion' in poetry effectively denies the possibility of any binary distinctions. In fact, crude and fine frequently exist side by side in the world's greatest literature, as even a cursory examination of Shakespeare will demonstrate. The true distinction is not between crude and fine (which is a simplistic classification of subject matter) but between good and bad writing (which requires a subtle exercise in literary discrimination). At his worst, for example, Layton could descend into something close to doggerel (which is crude in the literary-critical sense) while writing poems on serious and elevated topics. On the other hand, some of his most brilliant effects arose out of a supreme expression of crude subject matter that is no longer crude when he has transformed it by means of his art. I would offer as instances of the latter 'What Ulysses Said to Circe on the Beach at Aeaea' and 'O.B.E.' (formerly entitled 'Imperial'). At the same time, many of Layton's squibs, insults, and other jottings from a somewhat gamy experience have nothing in themselves to recommend them. They are, as it were, crude-crude rather than fine-crude: in these instances Layton had failed to discover the form or the words to achieve an artistic metamorphosis.

Unfortunately, it seems that a higher proportion of Layton's later work fell into this category. Perhaps the temptation to publish became greater in his later years; certainly the older Layton tried to gain some of his effects too easily. On the other hand, he was always an uneven poet, and certain critics have treated him unfairly by emphasizing his inferior work rather than his best (if a similar process were applied to Wordsworth, what reputation would he enjoy today?). If Layton's later work is less satisfying, however, it is partly because we have grown accustomed to him, partly because he tended to repeat himself. The kind of poem that shocked in a salutary way in the 1950s shocks no longer, and the age of permissiveness eventually left Layton with no obvious targets save the absurdity of the age of permissiveness itself. His most original work in the 1970s, however, has proved – characteristically – to be the most controversial: *For My Brother Jesus* (1976) and *The Covenant* (1977). Here we find him, more singlemindedly than ever before, pondering his Jewish heritage. The insistence on Jesus as Jew allows him, of course, to score some easy points off the more vulnerable Christians (as he half-admits in his foreword to *The Covenant*) but there is a passionate sincerity about the true poems – as distinct from the untransformed squibs – that gives a unifying substance and impressiveness to the whole. And the old verbal magic still operates, as in 'O Jerusalem' which begins: 'Jerusalem, you will be betrayed again and again.'

George Woodcock titled an excellent critical discussion of Layton's work 'A Grab at Proteus' (reprinted in Mayne), and there is certainly a sense in which he bursts Houdini-like out of any attempts to confine and contain him. Like Whitman, he contradicted himself and contained multitudes. He could be infuriating but, just as one begins to despair of him, he astonishes with an unforgettable rhythm or an original and stirring thought. X. J. Kennedy has argued that 'Layton is no thinker, but a passionate roarer' (qtd. in Mayne 211); it would be more accurate, however, to say that his thought was manifest within the roaring. He can easily be tempted to write beneath his best self (I wish he had realized that the peashooter and the kazoo are unsubtle instruments), but he produced some of the richest poems in Canadian literature: 'The Birth of Tragedy', 'For Mao Tse-Tung: A Meditation on Flies and Kings', 'Keine Lazarovitch (1870–1959)', 'A Tall Man Executes a Jig', and many more. It is his passionate realism that most endears; to adapt the title of one of his own poems, he recognized muck as muck but rejoiced in its fertility. He was a champion of 'carnal blessedness' ('Earth Goddess') and essentially a poet of life, praising in 'Against This Death' the body, the sun, and above all the human imagination

> scheming freedom
> from labour
> and stone.

Chapter 6

Plain Talk about Past and Present

In a review of *Poems for All the Annettes* (1962) George Bowering described Al Purdy as 'the leading poet of his generation in Canada as Irving Layton of his' (Davey ed., *Tish 1–19* 365). The assertion may have seemed premature at the time, but it has proved accurate. Purdy was only six years younger than Layton, and even published his first book, *The Enchanted Echo* (1944), a year before Layton's *Here and Now*, but he took much longer to find his true poetic voice. Even in *The Crafte So Longe to Lerne* (1959, contemporaneous with *A Red Carpet for the Sun*) the title was deceptive; although he had broken away from regular stanza patterns and the conventions of rhymed verse, he had not yet evolved the characteristic colloquial idiom that has come to be recognized as vintage Purdy. Or, to make the point another way, Alfred Purdy (imagine Walter Whitman!) was still in the process of transforming himself into plain Al. Not until *Poems for All the Annettes* (heavily revised in reprints, by the way) and especially *The Cariboo Horses* (1965) did the accents of the now well-known Purdy persona reveal themselves unmistakably.

Reviewing Layton's 1971 *Collected Poems*, Purdy revealed more about his own poetic practice when he remarked: 'As for metrics, they seem unimportant in 1971, merely an aspect of a craft whose most significant portion is content' (qtd. in Mayne ed., *Irving Layton* 204). Certainly, Purdy's best poems elude any metrical categorization, the lines fulfilling the requirements of emphatic speech, long and lumbering or short and staccato according to the mood being established. One may question, however, if content is as crucial as Purdy maintains; it is not so much the content as Purdy's often shifting response to the ostensible content that provides the true centre of any individual poem. 'Trees at the Arctic Circle' offers a convenient example. The title, underscored by the almost pedantic but surprisingly characteristic subtitle, '(*Salix Cordifolia* – Ground Willow)', indicates what I have called the ostensible content. But the main poetic interest lies elsewhere. Purdy begins by expressing a scornful response to their stunted condition ('Coward trees') but gradually, as he comes to understand the conditions they face, his mockery turns to admiration. He realizes he has been 'most foolish' in his judgments, and he makes a notable confession:

> I have been stupid in a poem
> I will not alter the poem
> but let the stupidity remain permanent
> as the trees are ...

The real subject is our tendency to make rash judgments out of ignorance, mistaking inadequate preconceptions for absolute principles; or, to go one step further, the poem is about Purdy in the process of changing his mind, offering himself as representative of all imperfect men.

But the scholarly subtitle has a further significance. It illustrates the extent to which Purdy under his 'ordinary guy' stance – his colloquialisms, carefully nurtured vulgarities, constant references to beer, booze, women, and sex – is a man of remarkable erudition. Learned Alfred, we might say, is never wholly submerged under joshing Al. This leads at times, I think, to an awkwardness within the poetry; an esoteric allusion may sound curiously out of place in a generally anti-intellectual setting, or a coarse phrase or reference appear exaggeratedly crude in the mouth of one who has just revealed himself as not only intelligent but highly sensitive. At the same time, however, this kind of unexpected juxtaposition is responsible for some of Purdy's best effects. In 'The Cariboo Horses', for example, we are offered a ranchy and even raunchy picture of uninhibited cowboys driving their wild mounts into the local settlement, but the narrator presents the scene against a larger equine panorama of

> Kiangs hauling undressed stone in the Nile Valley, ...
> Onagers racing thru Hither Asia and
> the last Quagga screaming in African highlands.

It is not the insight we expect from anyone in a position to observe such a scene, but it establishes an immediacy in striking continuity with a remote past.

This sense of living history distinguishes Purdy's work – not the grand events or (in themselves) the archival records, but the houses, artefacts, traditions, myths, and memories that keep the past alive in the present. A favourite device is the time-split, modern-day Cariboo horses juxtaposed with the extinct quagga. Similarly, in 'Potter' (*Cariboo Horses*) a modern Canadian craftsman producing commercial designs decorated with maple leaves and beavers reminds Purdy of anonymous Sumerian and Chinese potters whose work is now admired and preserved in art museums. But his most ambitious historical poetry is gathered together in *In Search of Owen Roblin* (1974), and conveniently illustrates the seemingly automatic way in which Purdy found himself enmeshed in history while building a house near Roblin Lake in the 1950s: 'I got interested in the place / I mean what the hell else could I do?' A latter-day pioneer, he thinks back to the original founder of the settlement whose name is enshrined in the name of the community itself. This long poem, adorned with photographs and a map, is a composite of many shorter poems that Purdy had written over a period of years and often published in earlier volumes. It does not, I think, represent him at his best – too often the tension slackens and the lines become limp; but it is of immense importance as the best-known example (because Purdy is Purdy) of the many attempts to do for Canadian localities what Williams had done for Paterson, New Jersey: not merely to re-create essential local history in verse but to record the process of recording.

Like Birney (and Layton), Purdy has been a traveller in various parts of the world – Japan, South Africa, Mexico, Cuba, the Galapagos Islands – and has written poems about his experiences. Unlike Birney, however, he is rarely at his best beyond the boundaries of his own country. This is, I think, because Birney can submerge his personality into his environment when taking a walk in Kyoto or observing native inhabitants in Bangkok or on a Delhi road, while Purdy inevitably writes about himself. When he visits the ancient sites in the Canadian north or the remains of Indian settlements, however, Purdy's imagination takes fire. 'If you have your own vision', he writes in 'Innuit' (*North of Summer*), the sight of an old Inuit carver can conjure up the 'race-soul' of his ancestors, and in the brilliant 'Lament for the Dorsets' the artefacts of an extinct people are enough to suggest a plausible and symbolically rich story about the last of the tribe. Here, as so often in Purdy's historical poems, past and present are subtly blended. The Dorsets, an early Artic people doomed by geographical changes they cannot comprehend, present mirror images of ourselves in a bewildering world ('What's wrong? What happened?'), and they are specifically compared with

> Twentieth-century people
> apartment dwellers
> executives of neon death ...

In 'Beothuck Indian Skeleton in Glass Case' (*Wild Grape Wine*) he can make a similar connection because, at six feet three inches, the Indian was 'the same height I am' and can be reconstituted in Purdy's own image. Thus he would

> never stand face to face with a girl
> and have to lie down with her
> to be properly friends ...

In this case, the persona of Al the womanizer assists the poem because it forces us to imagine the remote Indian from the massacred tribe as an ordinary human being like ourselves and so telescopes past and present, then and now. Purdy's historical imagination is not so much archaeological as atavistic; whether he is visiting Indian museums, the Viking site in Newfoundland, the battlefield at Batoche, or simply pottering around the cemetery near Roblin Lake, he is celebrating the ancestral dead who produced ourselves and our heritage.

Purdy is a poet of connections. Just as he explains the historical past as it impinges on the present, so he is himself an all-important link between poets like Birney and Layton on the one hand and younger writers like Alden Nowlan and John Newlove on the other. He reminded us (and it is something about which we need to be continually reminded) that poetry does not have to be solemn. 'Home-Made Beer', 'At the Quinte Hotel', and 'When I Sat Down to Play the Piano' (about the problems of defecating in the Arctic) are among the most hilarious poems in Canadian – perhaps in any – literature. But Purdy is most remarkable for his capacity to switch from the humorous to the profoundly serious at will, and he manages this by employing what the dust jacket for *In Search of Owen Roblin* calls 'the poetry of plain talk'.

After Purdy's revolt against the literary in the late 1950s, he avoided the conventionally rhetorical that Layton retained; instead, he cultivated a style so personal that it does not seem like a style at all. In the introduction to *Being Alive* (1978) he discusses his influences tongue-in-cheek, mentioning D. H. Lawrence as the most notable, then asserting: 'I think everyone influences me.' But in terms of language and rhythm he evolved a poetic voice that, while obviously North American, resembles no one's (though some younger poets have tried to copy it with disastrous results). He knew that language is the ultimate link between past and present but also that no two poets write the same language. His own has proved admirably suited to mediate between the contemporary world and a surviving historical tradition to which Purdy was (in the best Canadian sense) a Loyalist.

If Purdy, with his particular version of 'the poetry of plain talk', is the important stylistic innovator in contemporary Canadian verse, Margaret Atwood has been its dominating personality. Her laconic, tight-lipped poems in which violent subject matter is treated with a horrifyingly cool detachment represent something unique in our poetry though they have developed in orderly and traceable fashion out of Canadian literary tradition. Atwood is a graduate of Victoria College, University of Toronto, where she not only studied under Frye and Macpherson but soon encountered Avison and Reaney (both of whom she reviewed with precocious understanding in the college literary magazine). And her own early work – much of it scattered and uncollected, though a privately printed chapbook, *Double Persephone,* appeared in 1961 – is clearly mythopoeic. Such titles as 'The Triple Goddess', 'Childhood under Glass', 'Proserpine', and 'Persephone Departing' clearly indicate her links with the Toronto-based poets of the 1950s. What is lacking in her earlier mythopoeic poems is the characteristic Atwood tone and style. These qualities appear almost fully formed in *The Circle Game* (1966) which established her as a dauntingly accomplished poet, yet one cannot read very far in that book without encountering distinct traces of its immediate origins. 'This Is a Photograph of Me' and 'A Descent through the Carpet' present the basic pattern of descent below a 'surface' (the word occurs in both poems) to a hidden or alternative world; in other poems, enclosing maze-like rooms and isolated estranging islands are used with full awareness of their symbolic force. In the title poem it is not difficult to detect a combination of Macpherson's imagery and Reaney's subject matter that nevertheless emerges as pure Atwood.

Her mythopoeic origins enabled Atwood to construct her own poetic world out of material that was both native and cosmopolitan. The content is inevitably cosmopolitan, not merely because it derives its basic mythic structures from the Bible and Classical mythology but because the symbols and meanings upon which it draws have been shown to be 'archetypal' and so to possess universal validity. But this material is mediated to Atwood through native examples – examples not confined to the mythopoeic group. Thus one poem in *The Circle Game* is entitled 'Eventual Proteus', and the reference, though ultimately to Homer's *Odyssey*, must surely have come via Smith's 'The Plot against Proteus'. Sandra Djwa has demonstrated that Atwood writes 'from within a continuum of Canadian poetry' (Davidson ed., 16), and shows how, especially in her preoccupations with a post-Darwinian Romanticism, her work takes its place within a discernible line from such poets as Pratt, F. R. Scott, and Birney.

But Atwood's poetry is, of course, Canadian in a much deeper sense. In poems like 'Migration: C.P.R.' and 'Journey to the Interior', the psychological and historical travels she presents are expressed in almost assertively Canadian terms which are by no means merely geographical. Similarly, 'A Place: Fragments' and 'Progressive Insanities of a Pioneer' – and, for that matter, her novel *Surfacing* (1972) – use imagery and allusions of Canadian origin to make cosmopolitan statements about human beings in their environment. This process comes to its climax in *The Journals of Susanna Moodie* (1970), where images and preoccupations established in earlier books come together in an extended poetic meditation. Here Atwood makes a descent into the nineteenth century to see the world through the eyes of an original settler, to rewrite prolix Mrs Moodie in clipped, terse Atwoodese, to create a complex double focus in which to provide not only a twentieth-century view of the past but a ghost-like nineteenth-century response to the present. The book represents Atwood's individualistic way of interpreting past and present. It is also a collection of poems that form a larger unity (in the manner of Macpherson's *The Boatman*); Atwood's own symbolic journey in time blends with Moodie's in space, and she comes to realize the capacities and limits of her own consciousness by temporarily appropriating Moodie's viewpoint – and, in turn, being taken over by it. At the end of the book the 'English' Mrs Moodie has been transformed into something approaching a Canadian *genius loci,* and through her Atwood as a modern-day 'double Persephone' has understood, deep within the land and herself, the complex fate of being both woman and Canadian.

Atwood's development as a poet, then, is reasonably straightforward. By the time she came to publish her first full-length volume she had abandoned the tight structure and the stanzaic and metrical conservatism of the older mythopoeic poets. But she maintained a deep interest in formal elements that unified poems within a book, though *The Journals of Susanna Moodie* is her only volume held together by a specially assumed persona. *You Are Happy* (1974), for example, revolves around the theme of transformation, and the 'Circe/Mud Poems', a sequence within the whole, draws upon the Homeric story of Odysseus and Circe and is the closest indication within her mature work of her mythopoeic beginnings. Elsewhere she has generally been content to rely on thematic, imagistic, and tonal links – words, symbols, concepts all repeating themselves to enforce connections between poem and poem. The polarities so evident in Reaney are important in her work, though she varies them tirelessly and employs them as means towards an independent insight rather than accepting them, like Reaney, as basic ways of looking at the world. So we have the binary structures (he/she, love/hate, subject/object, art/life, fantasy/reality, outer/inner) that provide conspicuous frameworks for her poems, and even (as in *The Animals in That Country,* 1968, and *Procedures for Underground,* 1970) for volumes. Again, individual images recur like leitmotifs from poem to poem and from book to book. In *The Circle Game,* for instance, both 'circle' and 'game' become powerful images, and others include image-clusters such as camera and photograph, window, glass, water. Sometimes an image casually explored earlier receives deeper attention later; thus a very early poem is titled 'The Siamese Twins' but the concept develops to become central to a sequence that gives its name to *Two-Headed Poems* (1978).

But it is the tone created by her pared-down language that especially characterizes an Atwood poem. The effect can be conveniently demonstrated by reference to 'It Is Dangerous to Read Newspapers', her poem on the McLuhanite theme of the global village created by modern electronic media. The opening stanza reads:

> When I was building neat
> castles in the sandbox,
> the hasty pits were
> filling with bulldozed corpses.

Historically, this reminds us that Atwood, born in 1939, came to consciousness in the period of Auschwitz, Belsen, and Dachau. Newspapers link the natural growth of the child with the unnatural horrors committed elsewhere on the earth's surface. They provide, one might say, a technological illustration of Donne's 'No man is an island ... I am involved in mankind'. But what makes Atwood's statement remarkable – indeed, unforgettable – is the deadpan monotone directness that seemingly accepts the situation as commonplace, to be expected. The poem appeared during the Vietnam War and was doubtless a contribution to the literature of protest. Vietnam lies, to employ Atwoodian terminology, under the surface, but characteristically the poem is double-edged. The tone in one way accentuates the horror but on another level suggests a strategic, dulled response – an attitude that enables the speaker to stay as sane as possible in an apparently insane world. It is, in short, a poem that catches an ambivalent feeling of desperation at the pulse of its time. Although Atwood is capable of startling metaphor, she employs such effects sparingly, with selective economy. Her language itself deliberately eschews the euphonious; it is conventionally pleasing in its own right, but – one thinks of Smith and some other Canadian predecessors – sharp, brittle, precise, efficient. Unlike so many of her contemporaries, however (and here once again Atwood displays her links with the mythopoeic group), she never uses colloquial language. Artifice is used to create an almost clinical linguistic detachment.

Atwood's later volumes, though as accomplished as ever, inevitably lack the sense of dazzling surprise that made the publication of her early books so exciting. As always she is sensitive to the psychological temperature of the moment. *Power Politics* (1971) focused sardonically on 'sexual politics', while *Two-Headed Poems,* arising out of the mood surrounding the Québec separatist crisis but also reflecting in personal terms the period following the birth of her daughter, combines feelings of union and separation, love and hate, into a complex balance. Atwood's range extends here to encompass a tenderness that we have not heard before, though it is fair to observe, I think, that her style continues much the same and is as yet ill-equipped to reflect this new emotional development. *True Stories* (1981) records more sharply, possibly in response to depressing economic and political climates, the contrast between private life and love on the one hand and world intrigue and violence on the other. A number of poems arise out of the same experience that lay behind the contemporaneous novel *Bodily Harm,* a reminder that Atwood's poetry and fiction have coincided throughout her career. But her inimitable use of language, with its poised yet keen-edged exactitude and firm control through pauses and line breaks, is still evident. Typically, in the poem sequence that shares its name with the whole volume, a word like 'lies' takes on crucial and often punning potency: 'The true story lies / among the other stories.' Within this bitter paradox Atwood's elusive poetic intricacy is both concealed and displayed.

As we draw closer to the present day, it becomes more difficult to isolate the most promising and significant of the contemporary poets. Without a reliable crystal ball, it is impossible to tell who will develop and mature, who will dramatically change course, who will remain as they are or even fall silent. Purdy and Atwood, both of whom came to prominence in the 1960s seem likely to retain their current reputations, but since their appearance at centre stage one has been aware more of remarkable poetic activity than of outstanding poetic practitioners. It seems wise, then, for the rest of this chapter, to consider the contemporaries and successors of Purdy and Atwood in groups according to the kind of poetry they tend to write. As my chapter title indicates, I detect a common concern for the relation between past and present, and a preference for direct language as the central features of modern Canadian poetry. But these are aspects of subject and approach that can be pursued by traditionalists as well as by the radical avant-garde. I shall begin with those who follow more conventional forms.

Because of their Loyalist heritage, the Maritimes can claim a long-established verse tradition that concentrates on what Roberts called 'unregarded things' ('Prologue' to *Songs of the Common Day*) and displays a language that might also be called a 'poetry of plain talk'. Although for the most part they have not attracted the attention that is their due, the most distinctive of the contemporary Maritime poets – Fred Cogswell, Elizabeth Brewster, Milton Acorn, Alden Nowlan – have, like Purdy (and, before Purdy, Pratt), searched for less drastic ways of bridging the gap between popular and high culture, between what the ordinary man or woman reads and what is exalted as literature.

Literary critics generally regard Fred Cogswell as a New Brunswick equivalent to E. A. Robinson, but this is to exaggerate United States influence and underestimate the native Maritime tradition. We shall do better to see his early, laconic, deceptively casual sonnets about New Brunswick villagers – 'Miss Maybee', 'George Ernst', 'Sam Stover', 'Deacon Johnson', and the rest – as songs of the common people, an extension of Roberts's example in *Songs of the Common Day*. While Roberts confined himself to Maritime landscape, Cogswell concentrated on its human denizens, their joys and sorrows, and especially their sins and frailties; but both offer quiet, technically sophisticated, and crisply effective verbal portraits. Cogswell was the most ostensibly traditional of the contemporary Maritime group: he preferred the older forms of sonnet and ballad, wrote comfortably in rhymed quatrains and couplets, but could produce a flexible yet always carefully controlled free verse if the occasion demanded. One of his tricks was to use traditional verse forms to encompass decidedly untraditional content. His villagers are a decidedly unpastoral lot, and anyone expecting to find rural innocence in his verse will be both disappointed and shocked. His subject matter divides readily into two parts: objective poems of description and/or narrative; and subjective, personal poems recording his day-by-day thoughts and feelings. In the latter one gets the impression of a quietly thoughtful but earthily realistic man whose verse arose naturally out of his everyday experience – there is no hint of the poet set apart from his neighbours. At the same time, he had a deep sense of the importance of the past; he was 'at odds / with this a-historic century', he tells us ('November 11, 1979'). Such poetry is usually at best minor and at worst excruciating, but Cogswell almost invariably managed to redeem the quotidian, to convert the trivial and ephemeral into the valid and universal.

Elizabeth Brewster enjoyed a rural New Brunswick childhood before moving across the length and breadth of Canada to find other places in which to live, work, and write, and her poetry, originally fostered by

Fiddlehead magazine and the poets around Fredericton, retains a strong Maritime flavour. *Lillooet* (1954), reprinted in *Passage of Summer* (1969), is a half-loving, half-satiric presentation of village life in rough-edged couplets revealing the influence of George Crabbe (on whom Brewster wrote her doctoral dissertation), but close in tone and attitude to Cogswell's early sonnets that appeared in the same year. Its anticipations of the 'local documentary' style that became so characteristic a feature of Canadian verse two decades later illustrate her unostentatious originality. The impress of her native province is discernible throughout her work, partly because autobiographical reminiscence provides her with much of her subject matter. She may be writing in Alberta or Saskatchewan but her thoughts frequently transport her to the eastern seaboard. Nevertheless, although 'I remember' is a recurrent opening phrase, there is a saving honesty in her nostalgia. She employs sharp-eyed observation, as in her portrait of 'Aunt Rebecca', 'swift as silk and tough as the thin wire / They use for snaring rabbits', and this same combination of qualities is a typical feature of her verse.

Her later work refines and perfects her own style without showing any significant development. Writing readily of what she sees and feels in everyday situations, she can create poetry out of what might otherwise seem drab monotony, and has a remarkable ability to universalize her own modest experience. Her poems are generally short, intimate in their frank directness, and written increasingly in a carefully modulated and admirably supple free verse. Hers is essentially a poetry of understatement unified by tonal balance. Though individual poems vary in mood, they communicate her own vision; they are 'separate but wearing the parental features' ('Biography and the Poet'). It is typical of her that she should write a humorous, firm, but quiet poem about the tendency of critics to employ the word 'quiet' when describing her work. Because of this quietness, her voice (like that of so many Maritime poets) can easily be muffled by the stentorian shouts and apocalyptic screams of a noisy age, yet it leaves a lasting impression. Brewster's skillful combination of the nostalgic with the witty and comic, her ability to blend wryness with unpretentious grace and good sense, is unusual and perhaps inimitable.

There is little point in writing much about Milton Acorn here, since this is a book about the continuities of cultural tradition and Acorn's main concern was to challenge the established tradition whenever and wherever he encountered it. An avowed Marxist-Leninist, he was one of the few working-class poets that Canada has produced, and almost certainly the most talented. Originally a carpenter, he carried a preoccupation with craftsmanship into the writing of verse. It would be fair to claim, however, that his working-class poetry varies in quality according to the relative emphasis placed on 'poetry' and on 'working-class'. In *I've Tasted My Blood* (1969), a selection of his verse chosen by Purdy, one is impressed by an engagingly fresh viewpoint on familiar subjects. Love of the natural world before industrial capitalism polluted it is a favourite topic. There is an almost imagistic clarity and sharpness – Livesay's influence, perhaps – in 'Blackfish Poem' (later enlarged to 'Whale Poem'), where he writes movingly of 'the black whales / circling like dancers', and in the delicately rendered 'Hummingbird':

> its raspberry-stone
> heart winked fast in
> a thumbnail of breast.

But the latter poem is altered (and spoiled) in *The Island Means Minago* (1973), a revisionist verse history of his native Prince Edward Island, by the insertion of a trite political message. Indeed, as Acorn's poetic career developed, we find fewer of the sympathetic and effective poems about working people ('Callum', for instance) and more of the predictable chip-on-the-shoulderish rhetoric about mistreatment of the masses. Moreover, Acorn's later poetry seems less carefully crafted, more shrilly assertive. It stands proudly and abrasively outside the mainstream – but should not be neglected for that reason.

With the work of Alden Nowlan we encounter a particularly dramatic and engaging example of 'the poetry of plain talk'. Cogswell was his first poetic mentor, and many of his earlier poems, like the much-anthologized 'Warren Pryor' and 'Carl', bear a family resemblance to Cogswell's sonnets about representative Maritimers. But Nowlan had to come to terms with a harsher brand of puritanism than most of his fellows; his detachment in these poems is not so much an artistic method as a personal declaration of independence. Yet this detachment was also, one suspects, a calculated avoidance of self-revelation. His great breakthrough into personal and artistic maturity occurred when, sometime around the publication of *Bread, Wine and Salt* (1967), he was able to write poetry freely and unselfconsciously about himself.

This development is paralleled by the evolution of a colloquial style that conveys a corresponding relaxation of tone. What most impresses is Nowlan's enthusiasm and interest in everything around him. Many of the Maritime poets possess the capacity to make good poems out of ephemeral private or domestic moments, but Nowlan can outdo all the rest in this respect. His later books are all dedicated to his wife and son, and often to various friends as well, and one feels a joyous sense of a strongly knit family group emanating a friendliness that spreads out from relatives to chance acquaintances and ultimately to his readers. His poetry is full of the 'supremely human gestúre' ('He visits the shrine of a saint'). Moreover, he soon developed the ability to laugh at himself. So 'He raids the refrigerator' begins, 'Nowlan, you maudlin boob', recalling Purdy's setting down his stupidity in a poem, while 'He reflects upon his own stupidity', after he decides he is not alone in this condition, ends: 'I have found my tribe and am more at home in the world.' But the book-title *Between Tears and Laughter* (1971) indicates a basic ambivalence in Nowlan. He can be lighthearted, boisterous, indignant, tender, ostensibly casual, but he invariably introduces a sense of *lachrymae rerum*.

This combination of joyousness and sadness carries over into the impressive but frequently troubling poems, such as 'The Bull Moose', 'The Mysterious Naked Man', and 'The Visitor', that have become Nowlan's hallmark. These take the form of semi-narrative, generally open-ended, enigmatic myths containing what Dudek has well described as 'a sporadic symbolism drawn from reality' (*Selected Essays* 173). They always begin with the natural – 'Until then it had been such an ordinary day' is the appropriate title and opening of one of them – but they end in surrealistic fantasy, disturbing ambiguity, or the oddity of the unexplained. The poet refuses to insist upon a fixed meaning and leaves readers to provide their own interpretations.

The pattern of Nowlan's development, then, was from critical detachment to an acutely personal verse and ultimately to a poised many-sidedness that could contain both. Nowlan learned to know himself. The relaxed quality in his verse represents a hard-won victory over circumstances, and it exists only because some of the worst ghosts of his past had begun to fade. He had an *odi-et-amo* relationship with his own personal history. To remember was not generally a pleasure as it is for Brewster. Nevertheless, his poems are rarely bitter – or, rather, the bitterness is tempered with compassion and love. Thus in 'A Pinch of Dust', about a scrap of earth from the battlefield of Culloden where his ancestors 'were ploughed into / the compost-bed of history', he realizes that his past is only superficially represented by the physical object; more profoundly, it is within himself, 'a part of the very cells that shape this poem'. Nowlan's poetry is invariably concerned with the shaping of present or past experience.

Of all the Maritime poets since Pratt, Nowlan was the most adept at avoiding the limitations of regionalism while continuing to draw upon its strengths. His poetry is rooted but never stagnant. The abundant humanity that radiates from his work, whether prose or verse (though not always evident in the man), breaks all barriers and eludes all categories. Basically, he is as 'working-class' as Acorn, and poems like 'It's good to be here' say at least as much about social conditions and injustice as Acorn's but say it less explicitly and – for better or worse – with far more forbearance. 'It's good to be here'! Nowlan redeems the cliché and makes it sum up his characteristic attitude to life; 'how unthinkable it would have been', he writes in 'In praise of the great bull walrus', 'to have missed all this / by not being born.' The dominant tone we carry away from Nowlan's work is one of healthy and grateful celebration.

With most of the Maritimes poets one is aware of a social group about which the poems are written and to which they are generally directed. Brewster, perhaps because she has spent so much of her life away from her native region, may be an exception, yet for the most part her introspective poems present an agreeable solitariness that is known to be shared with others. But the anguished sense of individual loneliness seemingly inseparable from twentieth-century experience is also explored by contemporary Canadian poets, and Douglas Lochhead represents a notable Maritime instance. He is the most personal and elusive of poets, his voice often seeming no more than a whisper overheard. His poems are intensely apolitical, yet the strain of avoiding the political regularly breaks through; they are also asocial, though in an existential, not a communally irresponsible sense. While communicating a vivid impression of his environment, Lochhead speaks only for himself; he conveys a sense of landscape, weather, birds, but also of loneliness, discontent, loss. Many of his titles testify to his love of the outdoors – 'Into the marsh', 'In the summer woods', and the numerous bird-poems – but as scholar (moreover, as a scholar of Canadian culture) he has a deep understanding of tradition. Appropriately, the title of his collected poems, *The Full Furnace* (1975), derives from Lampman, while *High Marsh Road* (1980) is haunted by the spirit of Roberts.

High Marsh Road, in which his bird-watching meditative persona comes to the fore, represents his finest achievement. It is presented as a verse diary extending day by day over three months of the declining year. The tone is clipped, fragmented, enigmatic, his syntax dissolving as the natural images blend into each other. The whole of human experience is reduced to the solitary poet pacing the generally deserted Tantramar Marshes, and the poem's form arises from the related thoughts that the landscape inspires. In this area intersected with dykes cut by the Acadians and dotted with the toy-like barns built by early farmers, the past is both strong and close:

> there *is*
> a sense of history here and all across
> this marsh.
>
> (September 2)

Lochhead's emphasis is on personal – even, perhaps, psychological – history, represented by the shadowy figure of 'dear x', once a partner in what appears to have been a not-quite-achieved love affair. This is not a colloquial poetry but it conveys an individual human voice. Even if we do not share all Lochhead's attitudes and interests, we can respect the accuracy with which he records the mind's debate with itself; his soliloquies link with the inner, sometimes desperate meditations of us all.

The mature work of Phyllis Webb, a British Columbia poet, carries this candid desperation to deeper levels. 'Knowing that everything is wrong', she writes in 'Lament', 'how can we go on giving birth ...?' She began to publish as early as 1954, but the characteristic shape and tone of her poetry did not become clear until *The Sea Is Also a Garden* (1962). Starting within the international modernist tradition of writers like Page, she displayed verbal facility and an impressive if sometimes bewildering range of erudite allusion. But she soon learned to cast off her excess intellectual baggage, to pare down her language, to focus clear-sightedly on her own inner experience. 'Breaking', a seminal poem and one of her finest, faces up steadfastly to a world in which so much has been lost, but asserts a satisfaction in awareness of our condition: 'We would not raise our silly gods again ... / ... It is better so.' This poem is a magnificent *creative* expression of the condition of being 'absolutely broken'. A connoisseur of chaos, Webb knows that, although it may contain intimations of meaninglessness, a poem must reveal a form. Characteristically, a companion poem is entitled 'Making'.

Her poetry achieves its extreme of minimal expression in the impressively assured yet deeply disturbing *Naked Poems* (1965), poems that combine the directness of imagism with the enigmatic mystery of haiku. These are all

> Poems   naked
> in the sunlight
> on the floor,
>
> (Suite 2)

poems so private and fragile that, as with Livesay's contemporary lyrics, it seems almost an act of desecration to read them. Where, one wonders, could she go from there except into total silence? But after fifteen years she emerged again with *Wilson's Bowl* (1980), where she moves out (or back) to a fuller poetic speech and wider concerns (poems about 'divine paranoids' such as Dostoevsky, Pound, and Rilke, and the title sequence that grew out of a friendship with a woman who committed suicide) yet remains frighteningly subjective. That the language is limpid, restrained, serene, renders the effect no less chilling. We are aware in all her finest poetry of a mind desperately trying to maintain balance as the earth moves frighteningly underfoot, a mind pushing towards the extremes into areas of perception both fascinating and dangerous. Yet her verse proclaims a poetic order heroically against the flux, and *Wilson's Bowl* ends in a hard-won serenity that is both impressive and exalting.

Webb had begun writing before the literary nationalism of the 1960s had got under way, so it is not surprising that this striking phenomenon left little impress upon her work. Atwood has remarked that, when she was herself an undergraduate in the late 1950s, she felt no sense of Canadian literature or tradition (*Second Words* 381). Some rhetorical heightening may be present here, but it is certainly true that the 1960s saw an explosion of interest in things Canadian, including a growing awareness of the country's literature and its cultural and historic past. There were many reasons for this development, not least of which was the escalating rate of change at a time when remnants of this past were in danger of being obliterated. Other factors include a growing nationalism in response to the increased influence of the neighbouring United States as a world power, the opening of new universities, the curiosity of recent immigrants from various ethnic backgrounds concerning the land which they had made their home, the eventual impact of the historical writings of men like Donald Creighton and W. L. Morton, the establishment of the Canada Council, and, in terms of literature, the launching of the New Canadian Library and the magazine *Canadian Literature*. All these elements and many others – especially the need to make plans for celebrating the centenary of Confederation in 1967 – combined to produce a new national awakening.

It was a period of much excitement among young writers suddenly becoming aware of a stimulating heritage, and they responded, predictably, in a variety of ways. One poet who viewed the contemporary situation with decidedly less than euphoria was Dennis Lee, who had attended Victoria College with Atwood and collaborated with her in college publications. Lee was impressed less with the material and cultural boom than with the price that was being paid for it; he was particularly influenced by George Grant's philosophical broodings on national ill-being in *Lament for a Nation* (1965). Lee's poetic response was *Civil Elegies* (1968, revised and expanded 1972) in which, as well as debts to Eliot and Rilke, we can discern links with a tradition of 'meditative quest' (Pearce interview 50) going back to D. C. Scott's 'The Height of Land' and most notable in the work of Dudek. But where Scott observed a geographical Canada from a watershed on the Canadian Shield, Lee's twentieth-century vantage point was the recently constructed square in front of the new Toronto City Hall. It is a poignant threnody for 'a civil habitation that / is human, and our own' (Elegy 1, 1972), but it becomes a dour presentation of sell-outs and failed opportunities: 'we are the evidence / for downward momentum' (Elegy 3, 1972). For Lee both past and present are void; indeed, the word 'void' tolls like a bell through the whole sequence. Technically, the poem seems 'free', even periodically arbitrary in its seemingly casual mixture of long and short lines, but throughout there is a recurring suggestion of Latin hexameters which give a hint of both civic and poetic non-Canadian ancestors (the dedication is 'pro patria'), while tonally we are made aware of the Old Testament prophets: 'and I ran in my mind crying humiliation upon my country' (Elegy 5, 1972). Lee's language is poised between prose and verse, a characteristic developed in – even, indeed, becoming the subject of – 'The Death of Harold Ladoo' (1976, revised in *The Gods*, 1979).

This poem arose out of the murder while on a visit to his homeland of a young Trinidadian writer who had published novels with Lee's House of Anansi Press. It begins from an impulse towards formal elegy but ends as an autopsy on Lee's past self, and it demonstrates how so much of his writing is 'a refusal of poetry' (Pearce interview 46). He considers the flamboyant gesture of poetry in response to a death inadequate, even insulting. Moreover, he finds the conventional *de mortuis nil nisi bonum* (only speak well of the dead) constricting in any attempt to portray the whole man. His struggles with his ambiguous memories of Ladoo become an analysis of motives and responses (both poet's and subject's) only communicable through subtly modulated tones of verse and voice. Lee modestly describes himself as 'unendowed / with Muse or Holy Ghost' (I, 1979); instead, he constructs his lines laboriously out of his own sense of delicate language-variations. His is 'plain talk' modified for the purpose of serious meditation so that it can express a sense of loss – of a friend like Ladoo, of civic honour, and especially of a world of religious certainties. Lee articulates 'the need in extremis to be' (I, 1979). His later work has concentrated on children's literature written for the children always evident on the edges of his poems (his verse seems composed invariably to the sound of children shouting at play), and is a product of his civil and civic self. His shorter adult poems are, I think, less successful than his extended meditations, but some of his ballads – especially '1838' and the superb 'When I Went Up to Rosedale' – are rhythmically influenced, one suspects, by his poetry for young people.

The variety of subject, tone, and stylistic approach in John Newlove's poetry, though impressive, can initially be a barrier to appreciation. Sometimes, in poems like 'The Double-Headed Snake' and 'America', he wrote with Lee-like direct statement; more frequently, he was impersonal, communicating enigmatically through an impressionistic juxtaposition of images. Tonally the poems often seem pessimistic – Atwood lists his typical stances as 'revulsion, guilt, fright and paralysis' (*Second Words* 117) – yet his best-known poem, 'The Pride', is surprisingly positive in its final affirmation. And his subject matter shifts from vividly etched pictures of the prairies ('Verigin, Moving In Alone', 'Ride Off Any Horizon') through numerous poems about travellers, hitch-hikers, hoboes on the move, to the historical poems involving Samuel Hearne, Riel, and the Indian wars. All are united, however, by the theme of discovery within history, whether explorers (notably Hearne and Thompson) map out the contours of a new land in the past or Newlove (or, rather, the restless persona in his poems) moves from prairies to mountains to seacoast in the present. Certainly they are linked by a historical obsession. 'I'm interested almost to the point of violence in history', he confessed in an interview; 'I suppose I read history eight or ten hours a day' (Pearce interview 115, 122). In some respects the pessimism derives from this – history is a nightmare from which Newlove cannot wake up – but it is also a buttress, almost an inspiration.

In Newlove's work, especially in a number of poems from *Black Night Window* (1968), we can watch items from the Canadian past forming themselves into a coherent tradition. The past becomes present, blends with it. Thus the eighteenth-century explorer in 'Samuel Hearne in Wintertime' is as immediate for the narrator as his own personal surroundings:

> One child is back from the doctor's while
> the other one wanders around in dirty pants
> and I think of Samuel Hearne and the land.

A rapport is established via cold and fear; the poet's effort to understand Hearne revitalizes him, makes him contemporary. Similarly, a deliberate intention in 'The Pride' is to make Indian legend and story available for the modern Canadian consciousness. We are bombarded by fragmented and at first mysterious 'images' that eventually form 'the grand poem / of our land'. Like many modern writers (and especially Rudy Wiebe) Newlove was aware of the split between the land's past and the past of the people now inhabiting it, but he believed that an imaginative integration was possible. The Indians 'still ride the soil / in us'; moreover, 'we become them'. The poem is a deeply moving, though in hindsight over-optimistic, demonstration of this process, and its success in enlarging our historical horizons is attested by the fact that its central lines,

> the knowledge of
> our origins, and where
> we are in truth,
> whose land this is
> and is to be,

(Part 6)

become the epigraph to Wiebe's novel *The Blue Mountains of China* (1970). In such ways the Canadian literary and imaginative tradition gradually but doggedly became recognized and established.

Newlove's material is so fascinating and so significant that it is easy to overlook his considerable technical expertise. He is one of the most meticulous of contemporary poets in revising and improving his poems. Like Lee, he is conversational without being slangily colloquial; he can display both compassion and empathy for ordinary people ('The Fat Man') and for derelicts ('Company', 'Harry, 1967'); he can use their language, but he also transforms it. Yet throughout his work, and especially in his historical poems, he shows an extraordinary capacity to produce the memorable and resonant statement.

Of the many accomplished but relatively straightforward contemporary poets, mention must be made of Patrick Lane, who has not only built up a substantial corpus of fine verse over the years but has begun to write impressive and hauntingly cryptic poems that hint at deeper insights. His earlier work is a poetry not so much of plain talk as of plain statement. Most successful when it offers straight transcripts of working-day experiences, generally harsh and uncompromising, on ranches and in logging camps, it derives a special Purdy-like interest from the fact that the incidents recorded are rarely witnessed by those likely to write verse. The life of physical action is presented in the raw:

> I never learned

how to be gentle, and the country
I lived in was hard …

('Because I Never Learned')

But, although our first impression is of a tough and violent world, we soon become aware of a deep compassion behind the no-nonsense directness. This is sometimes explicit – the speaker weeps as his companions kill the marauders in 'Wild Dogs' – but more often unstated yet palpable. In 'For Ten Years' all he needs to say about the dead bird found outside the window is: 'Birds don't understand windows. / They never did.' At the same time, he knows only too well that 'compassion is only the beginning of suffering' ('At the Edge of the Jungle'). Some of the stark, dark subject matter is, I think, unredeemable (whatever fashionable theories may say) but surprisingly often it is transfigured into a terrible beauty.

His more recent poetry is dark in another sense. It is concerned less with daylight activity than with the enigmatic workings of the subconscious; it becomes a poetry of dreams and nightmare, of 'what runs underneath' ('And Say of What You See in the Dark'). This side of Lane's work finds its most eloquent expression in 'Albino Pheasants' where the night-birds seem 'as if they had been born in caves' and had 'risen from the earth' for mysterious purpose. They are beautiful but threatening, their ambiguous ways summed up in the unforgettable last line: 'Albino birds, pale sisters, succubi.' Lane's once straightforward verse develops, then, into poetry of symbolic, even mythic grandeur. The language remains simple and direct but takes on intensity and resonance. In the books published from *Albino Pheasants* (1977) onwards, Lane has opened up a whole new dimension of poetic reference which has made his work, with that of Robert Kroetsch, some of the most exciting Canadian poetry to have emerged in recent years.

The most recent experimental Canadian poets, though manifesting much variety, are unified by certain overriding characteristics. Perhaps the most obvious of these is an anti-humanist stance, a determination to challenge traditional modes of perception. This often involves a hostility to accepted methods of expression, the sanctioned norms of grammar, spelling, punctuation, typographical conventions, ordered syntax, and even the process of rational thought, in the belief that these constrict human awareness of, and participation in, the larger world of the senses and the imagination. Such assumptions are unlikely to coexist with any strong sense of cultural continuity, so I shall consider them only briefly here. But individuals do not think and create in a vacuum, and alongside the rejection of traditional values runs an openness to so-called 'popular culture' as providing a new context for poetic creation. Cohen's later career as pop singer is, of course, central here, but one thinks also of attempts to combine poetry and sound, the blending of verse with graphic design in 'concrete poetry', the preoccupation of Michael Ondaatje, himself a film-maker, with the photographic and cinematic, and poems like George Bowering's 'Radio Jazz'. The tendency is understandable yet disturbing. Against the commendable attempt to bring poetry out of its category of 'minority culture', to reunite poetry and the people (itself a Canadian tradition established by Livesay and Acorn) must be set the danger of underestimating the deleterious effects of associating serious poetry with the ephemeral, the commercially vulgar, and the notorious vagaries of fashion.

Other aspects of contemporary poetry, however, are by no means irreconcilable with earlier trends. One, that we have already seen employed by Purdy and in Lee's 'Death of Harold Ladoo', is an emphasis on the mind in process, shifting and developing as it responds to external phenomena. Another, a result of the swing away from personal lyricism, is an increased interest in long poems involving subjects that combine local history and documentary. Ultimately, the shadow of Williams's *Paterson* hangs over many of these, and the breakdown of the traditional separation of prose and verse leads to the long trailing lines of Daphne Marlatt's *Steveston* (1973), which unites poetic meditation with photographic images and sociological inquiry, and the collage effects in Don Gutteridge's *True History of Lambton County* (1977), which also incorporates newspaper cuttings and extracts from taped interviews. Moreover, many such poems continue the tradition of discovering and re-creating Canadian history, examples including Gutteridge's tetralogy of poems, *Riel* (1968), *Coppermine* (1973), *Borderlands* (1975), and *Tecumseh* (1976), David Helwig's *Atlantic Crossings* (1974), and Bowering's fascination in both poetry and fiction with the figure of George Vancouver.

Although his work reveals surprising links with earlier Canadian verse traditions, Michael Ondaatje is coming to be recognized as a representative and central figure in this new verse. In 'The Diverse Causes', for example, he notes the extraordinary bombardment of our senses by new technological inventions:

> We are in a cell of civilised magic.
> Stravinsky roars at breakfast,
> our milk is powdered.

Ondaatje offers an alternative way of looking; realism gives way to surrealism – and often, indeed, to horror. He is himself torn between the traditional aim of art to 'freeze this moment' ('Four Eyes') and a longing to record at least an illusion of movement, symbolized in 'The Gate in His Head' by the blurred photograph of a gull 'caught at the wrong moment'.

This image-blur doubtless connects with the intention behind Ondaatje's most substantial achievement in verse, *The Collected Works of Billy the Kid* (1970), one of the most successful and influential of contemporary long poems. Here we are invited to look at human characters in a new way. Moreover, despite the concern with photography, all is movement and flux. There is a perpetual blending of verse and prose, poetry and fiction (the later *Coming Through Slaughter*, 1976, is officially classified as a novel but employs many of the techniques of *Billy the Kid*). Contrasting poems and prose sections are juxtaposed like cuts in a film. There is a moral concern, certainly, but it is deliberately complicated by an early reference to 'the moral of newspaper or gun'. Pat Garrett may be sane or insane; traditional distinctions appear questionable. Above all, Billy, as the title indicates, is presented as a mirror image of the artist – the artist as outlaw, presumably; why, Ondaatje asks himself in 'White Dwarfs',

> do I love most
> among my heroes those
> who sail to the perfect edge
> where there is no social fuel?

The book is subtitled 'Left-Handed Poems'; Billy always shoots with his left hand. The promised opening photograph of Billy is a blank, but the book ends with a snapshot of a child cowboy rumoured to be the poet himself, at any rate a kid posing as Billy. Ondaatje loves to construct a rich, intriguing but deceptive world in which (like the world we inhabit) nothing is quite what it seems.

Much of Ondaatje's work, however, represents not so much a break with the past as a continuation of the evolving Canadian tradition. He can create mythic stories out of his own personal history ('Letters & Other Worlds', for example) that, linked to his preoccupation with imagery of violence, imprisonment, and madness, would not seem out of place in the work of Mandel. His interest in extremity and popular culture explains his attraction to Cohen (about whom he has written a booklet). And there are occasions when his underplayed, cool verse recalls Atwood's. His poetry contains an orderly intellectual brooding over violence and chaos, and if there is something disturbing (to a traditionalist) about the subjects upon which he so often broods – the Billy the Kid comic-book western myth, the King Kong of Metro-Goldwyn-Mayer – it should be remembered that these are balanced by references to Philoctetes and Wallace Stevens. Once again the habitual conflicts in modern experience between gentle and horrific, sublime and ridiculous, ancient and contemporary, become a central focus of his art. Moreover, it is possible to be too solemn in discussing him. Many of his poems ('Notes for the Legend of Salad Woman', 'The Strange Case') are humorous, playful, and poised, while 'Dates' plays brilliant variations on the traditional dichotomy between art and nature. But whatever his subject, the force and (once one is tuned in to his wavelength) the immediacy of his best poetry is undeniable.

The most recent full-scale 'movement' in Canadian poetry has come from the group of young writers who founded the Vancouver magazine *Tish* – including George Bowering, Frank Davey, Lionel Kearns, and Fred Wah. *Tish* appeared intermittently between 1961 and 1969, though it ended sadly in a dribble of drugs and counterculture; but in its first eighteen months, under Davey's editorship, it became a youthful, brash, experimental Canadian beach-head for the 'projectivist' movement associated with Black Mountain College in the United States. Essentially a student venture (its snook-cocking anagram-title is symptomatic), it responded enthusiastically – perhaps uncritically – to the theory and practice of contemporary United States poets, notably Olson, Creeley, and Duncan. Reacting against what they took to be the rigid formalism of traditional art and the élitist aspects of modernism, rejecting the bias of traditional humanism in shaping what was observed according to the dictates of the reasoning mind, the Tishites submitted to the destructive element, embraced chaos, invited the natural wind to blow through them. In consequence, they advocated 'the correspondence between breath and line' (Davey ed., 97) and favoured a style that avoided ornament while blending simplicity with current slang.

All this was proclaimed as revolutionary but, as so often, most of it had happened before. In terms of Canadian tradition, one remembers Smith and F. R. Scott in the 1920s, Dudek and Souster in the 1940s; and one can go back, of course, to the continual rebellions against strict forms and 'poetic diction' in English literary tradition, especially Wordsworth and Coleridge. The Tishites, indeed, were nothing if not Romantics. They have often been criticized for turning to American models, and the attitudes presented (flaunted?) in *Tish* itself certainly invite this response. As we have seen, however, earlier Canadian movements also looked abroad for stimulation, whether to British or American sources. What is important is not so much the origin of inspiration as the use made of it. Certainly Bowering and Davey have subsequently demonstrated an intimate awareness of their Canadian heritage, and the movement itself owes much to a respectful but independent response to Dudek's poetry and thought (see Davey and Nichol's *Open Letter* Dudek issue). And ironically, Bowering's best-known poem – perhaps the finest poem to appear in *Tish* – is 'Grandfather', which irresistibly suggests Purdy and is in the mainstream of modern Canadian tradition; one might say, indeed, that it helped to enforce that tradition.

Like all student groups, the Tishites soon dispersed, went their separate ways, matured – or failed to mature – individually. The ultimate aesthetic and literary-historical importance of the movement is still uncertain. While the Tishites may have assimilated the Canadian tradition (or part of it), the converse has not yet happened. Aggressively modern in their allegiances, they brought much-needed publicity to the literary activity of the west coast and helped to challenge the intellectual dominance of eastern Canada. This was healthy. Yet, with the exception of Bowering himself, they are known more for their controversial youthful theories than for their achieved work. They constitute a movement but not *the* movement to which, in their bolder moments, they laid claim. Nevertheless, they alerted Canadian readers to alternative poetic approaches. As for Bowering, despite his preface to *Another Mouth* (1979) in which he holds a tongue-in-cheek dialogue with 'Canadian tradition', much of his later poetry, besides showing only occasional traces of his 'projectivist' origins, is almost ostentatiously Canadian in reference. In 'My Real True Canadian Prophecy Poem' he is perhaps only half ironical in asserting: 'My lifetime breathing will be a poem for these provinces.'

The poet who seems – at least at present – to have most effectively converted the 'postmodern' attitudes into poetry is Robert Kroetsch, who brings to his verse all the experience gained by establishing himself as a novelist (see Volume Two). He shares with the Tishites and other contemporaries an emphasis on process and a mistrust of fixity in any form, whether involving the self, morality, or the conventions of literature (which must be 'deconstructed' and transformed to become available for art – at least, for his art). His poems are the extensions of the attitudes that produced his novels. They begin with history and point towards the future of the human imagination, embodying all the characteristics of modern experimentation. 'Old Man Stories' imports into the English-speaking consciousness the tall-tale Blackfoot legends from southern Alberta. Kroetsch begins, then, with tradition, albeit a native one, but the literal field, where the stone hammer of 'Stone-Hammer Poems' is found, soon blends into an 'open-field' dialectic in the best modern way (to quote an old-fashioned poet) and his most important poems take place in an ongoing work of personal archaeology entitled *Field Notes.*

The Ledger (1975) and *Seed Catalogue* (1977) are perhaps the most original and inventive examples of the fashionable documentary poem. Taking as its starting point a nineteenth-century account book, *The Ledger* is a poem about shaping; the trees are shaped into logs, shingles, tables, and chairs – and ultimately into poems. But Kroetsch in a sense re-creates the past by skillfully shaping the poem itself into the form of a ledger ('I'll be damned / it balances'). And *Seed Catalogue,* which in the first edition was printed over a facsimile of an actual catalogue to create a palimpsest effect, appropriately evolves into a poem about growth (how do you grow a prairie town, a past, a poet?). While documents are incorporated into both poems, the emphasis is always on their transformation into a new order of words; a fresh tone is created by the language in which such documents are embedded. Because of their verbal poise and control, Kroetsch's poems seem to me more linguistically interesting than Gutteridge's – or even Ondaatje's *Billy the Kid.*

Kroetsch is always conspicuously present in his poems, reproducing and embodying the processes of thinking and making. Even more important, his delight in language is evident in his deliberate juxtaposing of high and low forms of speech, of the ponderous solemnity of the written word and the bubbling vitality of colloquial prairie idiom. In both these poems there is a wit evident in the structure, the verbal repetitions, even the physical layout of the words on the page. All these effects were carried over into the later poems in *Field Notes* (1981, now *Completed Field Notes,* 1989) where, characteristically, Kroetsch pushes his poetic impulse to deconstructing extremes, playing complex linguistic games with himself and his readers. Kroetsch the inveterate punster is prominent here, and recalls Joyce – 'putting Descartes before the hearse' ('The Silent Poet at Intermission') – reminding us that he may owe more to established modernism than he cares to admit. Certainly continuity is implicit in his delight in words. Whereas the Tishites, more concerned with breath-length than resonant sound, eschewed verbal ornamentation, Kroetsch revels in it. However puzzled we may be by his perhaps excessive intellectual high jinks, we can respond to his almost traditional sense of style.

It would be a mistake, however, to conclude an account of contemporary Canadian poetry on this albeit dazzling extreme. Certainly the experimentalists have recently received much publicity, but there are other poets writing confidently and well who do not accept 'post-modernist' assumptions. In terms of influences from abroad the pendulum has been swinging towards the United States for some time, but pendulums have a habit of reversing themselves; as soon as one extreme is reached, the attractions of the alternative direction become evident. So it is that writers such as Don Coles, Stephen Scobie, and David Solway have discovered liberating possibilities in styles and forms usually associated with the British (or, perhaps more accurately, European) tradition. Coles remains faithful to ordinary experience and the exercise of intelligence; he has once more found a place for wisdom in poetry. After a promising but uncertain start in *Sometimes All Over* (1975) he has blossomed with

Anniversaries (1979) and *The Prinzhorn Collection* (1982). The authoritative rhythms of maturity are discernible in his informal, quietly meditative lines full of unpretentious and unselfconscious references to traditional sages – Tolstoy, Ibsen, Rilke. He is not afraid to derive an unquestioned modernity from the European past. Scobie, a Scots immigrant, has explored the whole relation between New and Old World in *McAlmon's Chinese Opera* (1980), set in Paris, bringing to the documentary long poem a clarity and careful shaping that reflects traditional artistry. In his deceptively casual poetry he has found a middle ground between conventional and free verse that enables him to draw on the virtues of both. Solway, whose poetic masters include Yeats and Robert Graves, even uses rhyme and regular metres; his poems *look* shaped on the page. He is preoccupied with 'How to Stay Alive in a Barbarous Age', as one title has it. 'In Defence of Marriage' is an excellent example of his rueful humour, and the thoughtful but self-deprecating 'I' that sounds through these poems is splendidly controlled. The emphasis is invariably on poetic finish, a sanctioned shaping.

And these poets are in no way imitative. They have found their voices, voices just as Canadian as Kroetsch's or Bowering's or Ondaatje's. In both cases, outside influences have been assimilated, transformed into a new and distinctive combination. This poised balance between British and American models will ultimately be recognized as a quintessentially Canadian – and independent – stance. It is, moreover, an accurate reflection of the pattern derived from our newly discovered sense of history.

Part Three

Drama and Prose

Chapter 7

Drama

Drama in Canada, it must be stressed at the outset, is still in an early stage of development. There are numerous reasons – historical, geographical, and economic as well as cultural – why as a genre it has lagged behind poetry and fiction. Of all the arts it is most dependent upon popular acceptance. Poetry can circulate in a minority culture; in bookstores serious fiction can find a place alongside best-sellers since clusters of discriminating readers are spread across the country; but a play needs an assured, concentrated appeal before anyone will risk a production. Moreover, because the staging of plays normally requires a considerable number of people – scenery-painters, lighting technicians, costume- and property-makers, stagehands, front-of-house staff, as well as actors – drama belongs to well-populated communities, and until comparatively recently few such communities in Canada could support a resident theatre group.

Historically, it is true, we may be surprised at the numerous theatres and 'grand opera houses' built across the country in the years immediately following Confederation, but many of these soon failed, and the rest depended upon touring companies often of inferior quality and almost invariably from abroad. Moreover, all these factors combined to inhibit the production of skilled professional actors; only a handful could hope to gain a livelihood in their own country. And without Canadian actors, Canadian plays were unlikely to command a hearing. The expense of touring across vast distances meant that only surefire popular successes were likely to be attempted. When other Canadian genres began to develop in the 1920s, drama had to combat the challenge of the cinema and a generation later the coming of television. Radio opened up possibilities of employment for playwrights, but at the same time deflected them from serving the traditional stage. Add to all this the ethnic complexity of the Canadian population with its variety of origins, traditions, and languages, often combined with a deeply entrenched puritanism suspicious of drama as a morally undesirable art form, and we can readily understand why Louis Dudek saw Canada as 'an ill country for dramatic productions or for the creation of a genuine dramatic literature' (*Selected Essays* 322).

The early history of Canadian drama is especially dismal. The Victorian period showed theatrical vigour but little dramatic quality; melodrama and spectacle were the keys to popular success. At a more serious level the nineteenth-century predilection for high-minded moralizing and uplift, together with the practical problems already described, led with a sombre inevitability to that most dispiriting of dramatic subgenres, poetic closet drama. The best-known Canadian example is Charles Heavysege's *Saul* (1857), a sprawling, three-part, fifteen-act recreation of the biblical story. An earnest autodidact, Heavysege had a hit-or-miss gift for the evocative poetic line but little experience of either critical standards or dramatic technique; and he was totally devoid of a sense of humour. Scene follows scene with unimaginative deliberation. For every line of sublime effectiveness there are a dozen of doggerel absurdity. He attempts, perhaps unconsciously, a presentation of the romantic agony, but the sense of bathos is recurrent.

Charles Mair, who can claim the distinction of publishing the first substantial though aesthetically unimportant book of poetry in post-Confederation Canada, *Dreamland and Other Poems* (1868), also attempted closet drama in *Tecumseh* (1886). Somewhat more interesting and marginally more successful than *Saul*, it at least has the merit of exploring Canadian historical material in dramatic terms. Mair's attempt to portray the Indian leader as a tragic figure is laudable, but unfortunately his execution is almost as uneven as Heavysege's. Mair writes throughout in an unremitting and pedestrian blank verse that reads as Shakespearean pastiche or even parody, and is essentially undramatic. The play ranks with Sangster's poetry as a classic example of the inappropriateness of Old-World forms and language to New-World subjects.

The development of a Canadian stage drama was forced to depend at the beginning of the twentieth century on amateur enthusiasm and activity. In an age when entertainment generally had to be self-created, the lack of professional companies was at least a stimulus to local groups. In consequence, early Canadian playwrights concentrated on one-act plays with small casts and undemanding sets. In literary terms, these often seem unambitious and even trivial, but at least they began the process of dramatizing Canadian experience. Merrill Denison's 'Brothers in Arms', 'From Their Own Place', and 'The Weather Breeder' (all performed in the early 1920s and published in 1923) are amusing but not particularly subtle comedies that play gently with the stereotypes of wilderness or farm life. It is significant, however, that his more ambitious and serious full-length play, *Marsh Hay,* a dour story about the boredom and frustration of subsistence farming, though written and published at this time, was not performed until the outburst of dramatic activity in the 1970s. It is a workmanlike and often powerful story focused on the rhetorical question, 'Will you never learn nothin?' (Act 4). Denison was doubtless encouraged if not influenced by the theatrical revival achieved by dramatists in Ireland and the United States, but he could not emulate their verbal texture or dramatic technique. Although Michael Tait is probably accurate in calling *Marsh Hay* 'without question the best Canadian play of the decade' (LHC II, 146), Denison's presentation of ordinary characters and simple situations was always threatened by cliché in plotting and weakening repetition in language. The latter, amusingly effective in the comedies, fails in a serious context. Denison's importance in Canadian drama is considerable, but in terms of qualitative achievement he remains a minor figure.

Though irritatingly uneven in quality, the plays of Gwen Pharis Ringwood represent a far more substantial body of work, though this has only been clear since the publication of her *Collected Plays* in 1982. Ringwood became attracted to drama at the University of Alberta and immersed herself in all aspects of the theatre. She has acknowledged the influence of the early-twentieth-century Irish dramatists in pointing the way towards re-creating on stage the experience of Canadians leading rural and isolated lives. At the same time, the plays she wrote in the 1930s, the one-act 'Still Stands the House' (1938) and 'Pasque Flower' (1939), and the reworking of the latter as the full-length *Dark Harvest* (written 1939), inevitably put us in mind of the Canadian fiction tradition. Gerth Hansen in *Dark Harvest* is a Grove-like figure resembling Abe Spalding in *Fruits of the Earth,* and these early works recall Knister's short stories or those of Sinclair Ross. We find here the same concentration on the love-hate relationship between man and earth, a similar sense of authentic solidity, but frequently experience an uneasy feeling that the dramatic climax is an imperfect resolution of the deeper implications of the overall theme. Her later exploration of indigenous Indian material is also significant, though here her love of the Irish dramatists creates problems when rhythms derived from J. M. Synge ('It was a proud thing to be old and tell the stories') appear rather oddly in the mouths of Indians in 'Lament for Harmonica' (performed 1939).

Ringwood was an extremely competent dramatist with a sound technique who could produce varied effects with ease. Her difficulty was to integrate form with content. The spectre of the well-made play haunts her work, especially her endings, and this becomes a liability when she was attempting a realistic mode. She is decidedly at her weakest when she has a message to put across, and her social and political commentary is generally embarrassing. Her greatest strengths come through in comedy and in her unashamedly artificial plays where realism takes second place to fantasy. Examples of the comedy may be found in 'The Days May Be Long' (performed 1940) in which a young woman vainly endeavours to escape from her possessive mother, or 'Garage Sale' (1982) where a slight plot is sufficient for a warmly compassionate portrait of an ageing husband and wife. The fantasy is best represented by *Widger's Way* (written 1952), which seems to me Ringwood's finest achievement. It is an original, high-paced play which combines elements of farce, comedy, and satire. The plot is complicated, impossible, and little more than a vehicle for good acting and good fun. Poised between art and absurdity it invariably inclines towards the former, and demonstrates a sophistication and control rare in Canadian literature and especially in Canadian drama. Were our dramatic critics not obsessed with the socially relevant or the trendily daring, *Widger's Way* would have long since been recognized as a sparkling if brittle theatrical gem.

In some of her later work, Ringwood experimented with a poetic chorus in the manner of Greek drama, but her verse is somewhat flat, and although she gains a distancing effect the result is never wholly satisfactory. But her willingness to attempt anything and everything, though it may have led to a dissipating of talent, was part of her importance as a dramatic pioneer. She wrote plays for over four decades – tragedies, comedies, problem plays, satirical sketches, among others. Her determination was salutary as an example, and her mastery of her craft will, one hopes, ultimately be respected. She was in no way a great dramatist, and was least successful when trying hardest to be profound. The full extent of her work was not revealed until comparatively recently, and discriminations will have to be made, but there should always be a place in the Canadian theatre for her modest but unquestionable dramatic gift.

The Irish influence on Canadian drama continued with John Coulter, an Ulsterman who began his career as a playwright when living in Dublin before emigrating to Canada in 1936 and who once had a play performed at the Abbey Theatre. Coulter, then, was an emigrant split in his cultural allegiances; as a result, some of his plays look back to his native Ireland while others focus on subjects from Canadian history. Undoubtedly the most successful of the latter is *Riel* (performed 1950). Coulter was fascinated by Riel, whom he considered 'the tragic hero at the heart of the Canadian myth' (qtd. in Anthony 62), and wrote no less than three plays about him, one of which, *The Trial of Louis Riel* (1968) has been regularly performed with ritualistic historical appropriateness in the Regina courthouse.

But *Riel* itself is the most ambitious version, and is of interest because it abandons realism for an unlocalized stage; it is intended, as the introductory note states, 'for presentation in the Elizabethan manner'. A Scots settler named Rabbie functions as a kind of chorus character, and the play is so designed that a cast of twenty-five plays thirty-eight specified parts and numerous minor roles (a method Reaney was to adopt even more radically for *The Donnellys*). *Riel* is a chronicle play that tells its story straightforwardly. Using basic scenery, it obtains its effects by means of simple symbolic devices – the Union Jack kicked under a table (Act 1, Scenes 3, 12), the torn Proclamation (Act 1, Scenes 11, 12). There are tableaux, musical effects, and memorable visual images, including the historical detail of Riel's dressing in frock coat and moccasins (Act 1, Scene 2). Coulter unifies his story by the repetition of significant words like 'evil' and 'victory/victoire', and by imagistic references that foreshadow the final action, thus anticipating some of Wiebe's fictional effects in *The Scorched-Wood People*. *Riel* reflects some of the lumbering heaviness of traditional chronicle plays, and the language is serviceable rather than eloquent. It lacks the visionary heights of Wiebe's novel, but Coulter's stylizations are skillful and neat, while the dramatic qualities of the climax can hardly fail. Canada's first important play, it is also a work of genuine dramatic power.

Robertson Davies was the first writer to bring unquestioned verbal skills and intellectual originality to the service of Canadian drama. Significantly, before he began writing plays he had obtained a firm theatrical and practical grounding in all aspects of the theatre. While at Oxford he wrote a thesis on Shakespeare's boy actors, thus exploring the history of both drama as a form and acting as an art, and he went on to gain valuable experience both on- and backstage with the Old Vic Company in the season immediately preceding the Second World War. Thus he returned to his native country with personal familiarity of an established dramatic tradition. In Canada the Dominion Drama Festival (DDF) had been inaugurated in the 1930s in an attempt to foster and encourage dramatic activity, and it was within the DDF, and for the Peterborough Little Theatre, that Davies first participated as director and dramatist.

His early one-act plays such as 'Overlaid' (1948), with their simple plot lines and homely comedy, clearly belong with the work of Denison and early Ringwood. What distinguishes them is a firmer dramatic control, a subtler variation of language, and above all a profounder intellectual basis. In 'Overlaid' Pop's enthusiasm for opera, his dreams of both the culture and fleshpots of New York, and his emphasis on 'emotional undernourishment' are amusing in themselves, but part of a larger and wholly serious analysis of what Davies calls 'the intellectual climate of the country' (*At My Heart's Core & Overlaid* 111). Characteristically, the three characters in the play all have individual traits but also represent aspects of the Canadian consciousness: George Bailey, the average materialist and sensual man; Ethel, the narrow advocate of a religion that has turned sour; Pop, hungry for greater imaginative experience but uncertain how to acquire it. Beneath the comedy is a genuine pathos that touches deeper levels than the superficialities of plot, and makes a play of ideas out of what might have been no more than an entertaining pastime.

While 'Overlaid' gives at least an illusion of realism, 'Eros at Breakfast' (1949) illustrates Davies's *penchant* for imaginative exuberance, and anticipates his later experiments in theatrical fantasy. Subtitled 'a psychosomatic interlude', it presents a departmental office within the whole bureaucratic organization that regulates a man's body and soul. It is a witty, zany, but very intelligent play about the complex psychology of love, and it reminds us that, if we are to link Davies with any dramatic tradition, it must be to that initiated by George Bernard Shaw. Davies tried to play down his debt to Shaw, but it is evident in the way in which ideas are embodied in dramatic characters, in his relish for exposing the absurdities of his times, in the lucid and smooth-flowing rhetoric that makes up his dramatic speech, in a satisfying formal artifice, and above all in the creation of an imaginative world between the extremes of realism and total fantasy. Davies's theatre is an argumentative theatre full of intellectual debate and witty clashes of ideas in high-spirited argument, always leaning towards what is described in *Question Time* as 'a world of another reality' (Act 1).

Increased dramatic activity in Ontario at this time enabled Davies to attempt more ambitious full-length plays. *Fortune My Foe* (1948) and *At My Heart's Core* (1950) were performed in Peterborough and Kingston respectively, and three plays of the 1950s, *A Jig for the Gypsy* (1954), *Hunting Stuart* (performed 1955), and *General Confession* (written 1958), were written for the Toronto Crest Theatre, a professional repertory group. In these plays we discern the characteristic pattern of Davies's mature dramatic work. All blend realism (or the closest Davies ever comes to realism) with an element of wonder. In *Fortune My Foe* the latter is represented by Franz Szabo, a European puppeteer whose traditional and delicate art goes unappreciated in the New World, though many of the characters, like Pop in 'Overlaid,' show that they hunger for the imaginative sustenance he can provide. And in *At My Heart's Core,* a historical play about Susanna Moodie and Catharine Parr Traill, a Byronic figure complete with a whiff of Satan tempts the protagonists with larger dreams and ambitions, which in Moodie's case involve the world of art. Moreover, each play contains an important lord-of-misrule character (Buckety Murphy and Phelim Brady) who represent a disreputable but engaging resistance to the polite norms of society. As always Davies is a polished entertainer who offers amusement and the pleasures of watching the variety of civilized skills that comprise traditional drama, but he also provides food for thought and an opportunity for his audience to expand its horizons.

The later plays carry this development still further. Magic becomes a common ingredient, but a magic that reveals the realities of our world instead of allowing us to escape them. At the climax of *A Jig for the Gypsy* (which might be categorized as a Welsh *John Bull's Other Island*), a fortune-teller, a conjurer, and a poacher drink a toast, 'The Magic forever' (Act 3); together they represent a positive if unconventional alternative to the shabby politics dominating the plot. In *Hunting Stuart* two characters are taken back into the past to live out sections of their ancestors' lives. And in *General Confession* (a play that on one level evokes 'a realm of magic' (Act 2) and on another recalls the Shaw of '*In Good King Charles's Golden Days*') the protagonist – Casanova, no less – confronts not only his past but aspects of his psychological self.

Readers of Davies's novels will recognize in the subjects just cited elements that become major concerns in his fiction. But what is remarkable about the later plays is Davies's exploration of them in intensely theatrical terms. When Henry Benedict Stuart, an unimpressive Ottawa civil servant, temporarily becomes his illustrious ancestor Bonnie Prince Charlie, taking on royal authority (and to some extent even dignity), Davies creates a superb opportunity for a talented actor. Similarly, the actor playing Casanova in *General Confession* must play out the character's youthful past as well as his aged present, while those representing the three externalized aspects of himself ('the Comedy Company of the Psyche', to use a phrase from *The Manticore*, Part 2, Ch. 11) play a number of different roles in the charades in the second act. No Canadian writer before Davies had used the potentiality of the theatre so shrewdly and effectively.

By 1960 Davies seemed about to blossom forth as a prolific and important Canadian dramatist, but there were various reasons why this did not happen. First, a dramatization of *Leaven of Malice* failed on Broadway and discouraged him from concentrating all his efforts on the theatre; a little later, his appointment as first Master of Massey College, a college for especially gifted graduate students at the University of Toronto, entailed time-consuming duties and responsibilities, and later still his success as a novelist with the Deptford trilogy channelled his creative energies into other areas. As a result, his later dramatic output was small, the most important being *Question Time* (1975). This play begins freshly and inventively, and promises to develop into a witty and satirical look at Canadian politics. But it turns serious and even solemn as it raises issues of personal and national identity. It contains some impressive dramatic moments and its basic ideas obviously connect with the Jungian concerns that had produced *The Manticore* a few years earlier. The stage devices, however, in particular the parliamentary debate in which Peter

Macadam acts as both prime minister and leader of the opposition, seem confusing and clumsy. Oddly enough, the play comes perilously close to closet drama, the stage directions suggesting effects that could hardly be produced in most theatres. Moreover, its Canadian emphasis in this case proves limiting; *Question Time* never transcends the national situation to become a more universal comment on the relation between politics and the personal life.

Davies's plays are always elegantly written and meticulously constructed. Most, for reasons of formal pattern as well as practical economy, maintain unity of place, and in *Hunting Stuart* and *General Confession* the action is chronologically continuous. He consistently emphasized the importance of craft in play-writing; his plays were at least as well-made as Ringwood's, and in the special dramatic ethos he creates, the world of wonders celebrated in his novel about theatre folk, this is an advantage. As in his fiction, he chooses characters who, whatever their education and attitudes, can talk readily and effectively. In his notes to *At My Heart's Core* he insists that 'variations of accent and niceties of pronunciation are important', that the play 'is written to be *heard* as well as seen' (*At My Heart's Core & Overlaid* 118). Davies's most important contributions to the theatre are qualities that earlier Canadian dramatists tended to neglect: concern for dramatic speech, a theatrical intelligence – above all, a sense of style.

James Reaney is the first Canadian poet of any consequence to turn to the theatre, and he brings to it the whimsical but often powerful quirkiness that is so evident in his poems. Unlike Davies, he embarked on this new venture with little practical experience of drama; moreover, he began to write plays – ironically, just as professional Canadian theatre was expanding in scope – with a decided preference for the amateur stage. These factors account for the freshness and some of the weaknesses of his dramatic writing.

The Killdeer (1962, considerably revised 1972), *The Sun and the Moon* (1962), and *The Easter Egg* (performed 1962) conveniently represent his early phase. Like his early poetry they are full of references to rural southwestern Ontario but soon create their own strange world of fantasy and dark fairy tale, inhabited by egg-girls and comic clergymen, abortionists and diabolical sinners. In Reaney's theatrical never-never land of archetypal polarities, the pendulum swings constantly between a height-ened innocence verging on naivety and an evil-minded experience that on occasion seems little more than immature nastiness. Filled with quaint characters bearing names like Manatee and Kingbird, the plays also contain horrifying intimations of violence and cruelty, both physical and mental. The sympathetic characters, generally sensitive youths, are initially oppressed but always triumph through their faith in a redeeming imagination. There are drastic shifts of tone from rather obvious satire through melodramatic suspense to a resolution that often comes close to wish-fulfilment. Here, as in Reaney's poetry, we find what Dudek has called 'strange infantilism' and a 'regressive attachment to melodrama' (*Selected Essays* 324, 327). A 'let's pretend' attitude is all-pervasive.

These plays are written in a flexible and often haunting free verse possibly influenced by the revival of poetic drama in England a few years earlier. Reaney's imagery often dazzles like Christopher Fry's, and at other times the poetry is so muted as to recall T. S. Eliot's notorious method of writing dramatic verse that most of his audience would not recognize as such. Reaney's dramatic effects are poised on the razor's edge between imaginative charm and irritating silliness. While he frequently succeeds in establishing a poetic reality in which we are temporarily prepared to suspend disbelief, it rarely becomes more than an insubstantial pageant. There is an operatic quality about Reaney's plots, and it may not be acci-dental that the most consistently satisfying of his early dramatic ventures was his libretto for *Night-Blooming Cereus* (1962), written in collabo-ration with the composer John Beckwith.

In 1960, as he has noted on several occasions, Reaney attended a performance of the Peking Opera in Toronto, and this experience profoundly affected his own dramatic writing. It opened his eyes to the rich possibilities of mime and a consequent expanding of the audience's imagination; more practically, its dramatic artifice allowed for effects that could not otherwise be achieved on the stage. It freed him from the constraints and expense of elaborate stage sets and encouraged a dra-matic fluidity that fitted his own talents. As usual, however, there is an ambiguous oddity surrounding this development. The Peking Opera at that time was one of the most rigorously professional theatres in the world, its reputation built upon centuries of experience and training. Reaney proceeded to adapt their effects not merely for inexperienced amateurs but even for schoolchildren. The results, though original and stimulating, were hardly comparable with the model.

The first two plays to be notably influenced by this development were *Listen to the Wind* (performed 1966) and *Colours in the Dark* (performed 1967). Reaney now employs theatrical resources far more originally and imaginatively. In both a comparatively small cast plays a host of characters, and the former is grounded in a play-within-a-play situation. Both look back to the partly innocent, partly by-no-means-innocent world of childhood. In *Listen to the Wind* a group of children stage a play based on one of Rider Haggard's melodramatic novels. It is a play of intrigue, villainy, and infidelity, and the implicit motive for the performance is to bring together and reunite separated parents. The unhappy 'real' situation of the frame story (full of allusions to the Brontës' Haworth) is reflected in the tortured plot of the staged play. But Reaney's enthusiasm for what most readers consider crude and unsubtle melodrama raises problems. He merely asserts in the printed production notes that 'the patterns in it are not only sensational but deadly accurate'. Dudek, however, asked shrewdly 'whether it's good enough as a "pattern" of any deep meaning' (*Selected Essays* 328). Reaney's eulogizing critics never come to grips with this challenge, and the reader or spectator who shares Dudek's unease is likely to sense a dramatic failure here.

Colours in the Dark, which gave Reaney his first professional success when it was produced at the Stratford Festival during centennial year, offers a collage of dramatic and poetic images rather than a conventional plot. Structured upon a complicated and somewhat artificial division into the days of the week with their balancing planets, colours, flowers, parts of the alphabet, etc., the play absorbs some of Reaney's earlier published poems into a new imaginative context. Its subject is a child's developing view of the world, and Reaney himself has emphasized in an introductory note how it grew out of the idea of a play-box, a childhood image that has always been important in his poetry. Perhaps best described as a poetic revue, *Colours in the Dark* combines sentiment, chilling insight, archetypal patterning, quaintness, and fantasy into a theatrical potpourri that, whether one reacts with enthusiasm or reservation, is quintessentially Reaney.

But Reaney's chief claim to success as a dramatist rests upon the *Donnellys* trilogy, comprising *Sticks and Stones* (1975), *The St. Nicholas Hotel*

(1976), and *Handcuffs* (1977). Here his somewhat wayward dramatic talents are firmly grounded in a solid if mysterious historical event. Apparently part of an inter-Irish feud extending back for over a century, the murder of the Donnelly family in 1880 in Lucan, Ontario, not far from Reaney's Stratford, is one of the most sensational and unsolved crimes in Canadian history, and has taken on mythic overtones in the intervening years. Reaney dramatizes the story at length, and brings to his trilogy all the dramatic expertise he had developed during the previous decade. A series of recurring images – ladders, burning barns, and especially the sticks, stones, and handcuffs that appear in the titles – give unity of texture to both script and dramatic action; the plays are interspersed with ballads, songs, and other music; ingenious improvisations of dramatically intractable material dexterously turn liabilities into virtues. Above all, Reaney is able to maintain a tonal suspense in no way lessened by the audience's awareness of how the story must end. This is a dramatic subject explored with an abundance of theatrical audacity and inventiveness.

Nevertheless, although the historical/documentary aspect of the story constitutes a strength, its relation to Reaney's habitual procedures is by no means smooth. He never makes up his mind whether he is telling the truth (so far as it can be established) concerning the Donnellys or creating his own myth about them. If Thomas P. Kelley's sensationalist account, *The Black Donnellys* (1954), is in Reaney's own words 'viciously biased' (*Sticks and Stones*, Act 1), his own trilogy might be described as virtuously biased. He attempts to turn the Donnellys, so often portrayed as monsters, into heroic figures, and their opponents necessarily take on the role of villains. Reaney's notorious weakness for melodrama reveals itself in his polarized characterizations; the anti-Donnelly pact between Tories and ecclesiastics in *Handcuffs* seems especially crude. The binary groups to which Reaney seems addicted – here the sticks and the stones, the 'false' and the 'true' Donnellys – continually undermine his persuasiveness as an interpreter of the historical event. Although *The Donnellys* provides stirring theatre, it is hardly subtle.

Reaney's more recent plays, though developing his newly discovered ability to exploit local history, have been decidedly less successful. The poltergeist story re-created in *Baldoon* (1976, written in collaboration with C. H. Gervais) becomes a vehicle for many of Reaney's excesses and few of his strengths, while his claim to believe the story 'principally because it's a great deal more interesting to, than not' (author's note) hardly inspires confidence. As for *Wacousta!* (1979), it is even more melo-dramatic than Richardson's original and includes some surprising and embarrassing lapses in dialogue ('de Haldimar, you bastard. Give me back that girl', Act 3, Scene 5). All in all, it seems fair to suggest that Reaney has a superfluity of dramatic inventiveness but little tact; he is well endowed with vitality but sadly lacking in self-discipline and self-criticism. While in some ways an infuriating figure, he has certainly opened up exciting new possibilities for Canadian drama.

The last forty years or so have seen a remarkable flowering of Canadian literature in all forms, and, quantitatively speaking, drama has kept up with this development. There are now more theatres and actors, and as a result far more Canadian dramatists and plays. Whereas it was difficult in the not-too-distant past for Canadian plays to gain a hearing, the situa-tion has now changed so drastically that one dramatist, in an interview, claimed Canada as 'the easiest country in the world' in which 'to get a play produced' (Wallace and Zimmerman interview 153). This is not, of course, a situation that necessarily ensures quality, and any unbiased report is, I believe, forced to the conclusion that, for all the theatrical activity and publicity of recent years, the tally of plays that may reason-ably be expected to form part of a permanent repertory is still disappoint-ingly low.

Many reasons can be assembled to explain this sorry state of affairs. Theatrical awareness cannot be learned overnight, and many of our dramatists of the recent past lacked the basic experience upon which to build. Time and time again, young playwrights have displayed a depress-ing ignorance about the tradition of their craft. Thus one admitted to dis-covering Ibsen after he was himself a supposedly established playwright; another even recalled that 'the second live play I saw was one of mine' (Wallace and Zimmerman interview 111, 222). The absence of a developed Canadian dramatic tradition has been equally unfavourable. The modest comedies of Denison and Ringwood have little to offer the contemporary scene, while Davies and Reaney, our most distinguished playwrights to date, are both notoriously individualist, lone wolves so far as drama is concerned. They have discovered in theatre an outlet for their particular talents but, although many dramaturgical tips could be learned from them, they are of little use as formal models.

Moreover, this expansion came at a somewhat inopportune historical moment: the unsettled period of the late 1960s. Since it was obviously neglected, the theatre was a natural area in which radicals, often with more socio-political zeal than dramatic ability, could develop a subversive art form; according to one writer, for example, 'it is the theatre's job to outrage' (Wallace and Zimmerman interview 207). Drama, as an art that under favourable conditions could reach the people, had to be 'contemporary', 'relevant', 'committed'; and potentially dramatic, even explosive topics lay ready to hand. Drugs, violence, homosexuality, sexual perversion, madness, terrorism, feminism, exploitation of native peoples, the evils of capitalism: all these subjects could be used by the new drama to give an impression that it was a theatre not only of ideas but of advanced ideas. These are, of course, important issues, and could well provide subject matter for mature theatre. But too often play-writing became no more than a vehicle for propagandizing; the emphasis fell on 'message' rather than dramatic subtlety. Consequently, in line with democratic ideals, communal theatre became the order of the day. A surprising number of plays in this period (Reaney's *Donnellys* included) came into being as a result of co-operatives in which actors, director, and playwright pooled ideas and experimented with situations and dialogue to produce a collaborative effort. Many of these productions have been extremely effective on stage, and some dramatists (Reaney, presumably, included) have benefited from such experiences. But most have ultimately found the process frustrating, inhibiting the development of a personal style. It produced fine performances but few fine plays and fewer playwrights.

Above all, this was a period when verbal sensitivity was notably scarce. Playwrights more familiar with cinema and television than with the traditional stage are unlikely to develop an ear for eloquent or varied speech. The major weakness in most recent drama has been one of language. I refer not merely to what Davies calls 'shit-piss-fuck dialogue' (*Question Time* xi), which soon becomes tedious when over-used, but to the flatness and poverty of contemporary speech, the monotony of current idiom, and the decline of regional dialects. The mass media are doubtless to blame. One Canadian playwright was recorded as saying:

'Like many of my generation, my mind is like a sort of media garbage bag sometimes' (Rubin and Cranmer-Byng eds., 183). Neither the sentiment nor the expression is reassuring.

The work of George Ryga, whose *Ecstasy of Rita Joe* (1970) was one of the most popular Canadian plays in the 1970s and the 1980s, provides a good illustration of the pressures and urgencies confronting contemporary playwrights. His plays drew attention to significant modern issues – the treatment of Indians in 'Indian' (1962) and *Rita Joe,* the hippie phenomenon in *Grass and Wild Strawberries* (1971), and political terrorism in *Captives of the Faceless Drummer* (1971, clearly stimulated by the 1970 Montréal kidnappings). Even *Paracelsus* (1974) involves modern controversies like medicare and abortion. By concentrating on social-problem drama, Ryga inevitably risked the difficulties raised by all propagandist art. Thus *Grass and Wild Strawberries* has already dated badly, though *Captives* still retains interest, partly because terrorism is a continuing international concern, partly because the characters of terrorist and hostage become interesting in their own right, transcending the political attitudes that each represents. His establishment figures (the agent in 'Indian', the magistrate in *Rita Joe*) ultimately reveal themselves as straw men. *Paracelsus,* in particular, is crippled by black/white moral polarities. Rita Joe comes closest to becoming a genuinely dramatic, even tragic figure, but even she can lapse into a socio-political symbol.

Ryga used the stage imaginatively; his dramatic action often portrays the phantasmagoria within the characters' minds. *Rita Joe* certainly emanates a crude power, even if one feels that her dilemma is more moving than the play itself. The climactic rape-murder is a dramatically sensational ending that hardly concludes the political and intellectual argument that the play has set in motion. Although it is far less known, *Ploughmen of the Glacier* (1977), in which Beckett's influence is more evident than Brecht's, seems to me the more artistically successful because its subject – materialist greed within the context of other human drives and obsessions – is more universally philosophical than locally political, and the characters, though convincingly realized, are human types from which Ryga can keep dispassionately detached. Here, too, the dialogue is crisper. In his other works, by accepting 'the language and human qualification of the people to whom and for whom [a play] speaks' (*Ecstasy* 20), Ryga severely limited himself in the interests of his ideological position. Whatever their political merits, such sentiments can be a liability in the theatre.

Ryga was born in Alberta and wrote most of his plays about and for western Canada. One of the more positive effects of the recent dramatic expansion has been the appearance of plays from outside Ontario, which had previously claimed almost a monopoly on Canadian drama in English. One prairie writer who turned his attention to the theatre in these years was W. O. Mitchell, whose vitality of language and characterization was well suited to drama, though he did not achieve the depth of insight to be found in his best fiction. *Back to Beulah* (performed 1976) contains some remarkable psychological penetration but is hampered by a creaking plot. Elsewhere Mitchell's weakness for sentiment and whimsy intrudes. Though less ambitious than most, *The Black Bonspiel of Wullie MacCrimmon* (revised from a 1951 radio play), with its poised humour and delicate fantasy, is perhaps his most satisfying stage play.

Michael Cook, an English immigrant, managed to establish a well-deserved reputation as a dramatic interpreter of Newfoundland. Perhaps significantly, his theatrical work developed, like Mitchell's, out of radio drama, and he has spoken shrewdly of radio as 'the last refuge of the spoken word' (*Canadian Theatre Review* 36, 1982, 49). Cook's plays are varied in tone and reveal numerous external influences, but his sensitivity to language and rhythm distinguished him from most of his contemporaries. His historical plays, *Colour the Flesh the Colour of Dust* (1972), *On the Rim of the Curve* (1977), and *The Gayden Chronicles* (1977) all clearly derive from Brecht; the audience is kept detached, distanced, is encouraged to discriminate and come to firm social judgments. His didactic tone, however, like Ryga's, is often too shrill. The extermination of the Beothuck Indians was an appalling event, but it is difficult to see what purpose is served by its painful dramatization in *On the Rim of the Curve*. Other plays, including *Quiller* (1975), *Tiln* (first performed on radio 1971), and *Therese's Creed* (1977), with their queer blend of humour, pathos, and grotesquerie, owe much to Beckett, though a distinct flavour of Newfoundland life and attitudes is conveyed through both situation and dialect. Cook presented local characters displaying the spare bleakness of their lives while at the same time bearing witness to a universalizing humanity.

Cook's great virtue was that, while not afraid of outside influences, he was strong enough to absorb and transcend them. His finest work is to be found in the two half-realistic, half-symbolic plays that catch unforgettably the primitive Newfoundland fishing culture of the very recent past, *The Head, Guts and Soundbone Dance* (1974) and *Jacob's Wake* (1975). In the former especially, we find an extraordinarily assured blend of poignancy and humour, horror and regret. Above all, it is a play rooted in local speech and custom. We may be reminded of situations and dialogue in J. M. Synge, but Cook has created an authentic seaboard world which is hard, uncompromising, and abidingly human. An aged fisherman daydreams about a vanished past and so fails to come to terms with the encompassing present; the character of Skipper Pete is complex, arousing richly varied responses, and Cook subtly divides our moral judgments from our human sympathies. *Jacob's Wake* is a powerful study of the pressures that both unite and split a family, and it is by no means limiting to describe the play as a Newfoundland *Heartbreak House*. Weirdly effective – in some sense a tragedy but very funny on the way – it moves from naturalism to a supernatural near-allegory that is affecting even if it leaves the spectator somewhat uneasy.

But it is in David French's plays about the Mercer family, *Leaving Home* (1972) and *Of the Fields, Lately* (1973), that we find perhaps the two most accomplished plays in recent Canadian theatre. The Mercers are Newfoundlanders who moved west to a modest but more satisfactory life in Toronto. 'Leaving home' refers both to the parents leaving Newfoundland and their two sons moving out to begin new lives. Both plays dramatize the clash of generations and individual personalities. They are presented in a basically naturalistic mode, though French achieves special effects that are by no means limited to the conventions of verisimilitude; the figure of Harold in *Leaving Home,* who drinks but never speaks, is a delightful piece of dramatic artifice, and Wilf's account of seeing his wife's ghost in *Of the Fields, Lately* shows French's skill at making the unlikely acceptable. Moreover, the finely modulated dialogue and carefully orchestrated shifts between scenes of great intimacy and violent altercation are the work of a skilled and assured writer. These plays transcend locality to become tragicomedies of universal poignancy and effectiveness.

These two plays are drawn, in terms of the way of life presented, from

French's personal upbringing. And in a later play, *Jitters* (1980), he uses his professional experience in the theatre as the subject for brittle light comedy. *Jitters* is about a play being produced, the behind-stage rivalries, last-minute crises, first-night nerves, the absurdities, pettiness, and strange wonder of theatrical life. Both a parody and celebration of contemporary show business, it is in no way a profound play but a splendid piece of theatricality, expertly constructed and subtly paced. Though it could hardly be called surrealistic, the dramatic larger-than-life setting allows French the best of both worlds. It begins with a scene of naturalistic drama that turns out to be merely a rehearsal of a play-within-a-play, and the complexity of actors acting actors both on- and off-stage gives the play an additional, highly theatrical distinction. French is a dramatist who can be intelligent without making an obvious didactic point. He shows that experimentation is no substitute for depth of characterization and the pleasures of an artfully constructed play. His work demonstrates that solid dramatic skill is attainable in Canada, and sets a model – in quality if not in tone and style – for a healthy national drama in the future.

Chapter 8

Prose

Works of non-fiction prose are generally the last to be admitted (often grudgingly) into a nation's literature. Canada, like other countries, has produced fine examples of autobiography, biography, essays, and scholarship, and it is impossible to consider more than a tiny percentage here. It may not be a coincidence, however, that our non-fiction prose is distinguished by what could be classified as geographical and intellectual cartography. Such writing is both quantitatively and qualitatively conspicuous, and I shall therefore concentrate on prose of pioneering discovery, first of exterior and later of interior landscapes.

Despite ever-increasing urbanization, the Canadian land mass still contains a high proportion of wilderness, of uncultivated or uncultivatable land. It is hardly surprising, then, that a great deal of non-fiction in the twentieth century was preoccupied with the subject that dominated earlier writing: how to describe and encompass the terrain, to make it comprehensible in human terms. Most of this literature, factual and informative in character, is ephemeral and of no permanent interest. What initially concerns us here are the books that, while technically classifiable as non-fiction, attempt an imaginative re-creation of experience in the wild, books that endure only in part by virtue of their content, primarily because of the quality of their prose.

Frederick Philip Grove's *Over Prairie Trails* (1922) is a classic of the genre. In the winter of 1917–18 Grove was a high-school principal in Gladstone, Manitoba, while his wife ran a one-room schoolhouse in Falmouth, thirty-four miles away as the crow flies. The book purports to describe seven out of seventy-two drives (thirty-six each way) that Grove made by buggy or cutter during this period. I say 'purports' because we have no means of checking details, and the accounts, like Grove's other supposedly autobiographical writings, show signs of careful arrangement and patterning. Most probably they are composites highlighted with characteristic exaggeration to unite within an artful and effective design the most memorable and representative of his experiences; in private correspondence he described the book as 'about 1/4 fiction and 3/4 fact' (qtd. in Hjartarson ed., 115). Although its pages are studded with references to Thoreau, Burroughs, and 'Nature-Study cranks' (Ch. 5), in which category he includes himself, *Over Prairie Trails* is more an expression of human moods than of environmental conditions. We gain a vivid picture of Grove both combating the elements (the journeys are undertaken in darkness, fog, snow, wind, etc.) and analyzing himself in this same process. Details of the external world are mediated through a thoughtful, inquisitive, and creative consciousness. Drives are differentiated not so much by changes in conditions as by changes in Grove's inner attitude; the 'I' alters with the landscape and vice versa.

Above all, despite Grove's stylistic awkwardness in his fiction, here he commands an eloquent, harmonious, well-controlled prose; '"observing"', he notes, 'means to me as much finding words to express what I see as it means seeing itself' (Ch. 5). He aims 'to suggest rather than to describe' (Ch. 3). A style that convinces by its fidelity to the writer's mood, it is seen at its best in the climactic snow journey: 'I shall never forget the weird kind of astonishment when the fact came home to me that what snapped and crackled in the snow under the horses' hoofs, were the tops of trees' (Ch. 4). An account of action and struggle, of man pitting himself against the relentless forces of nature, *Over Prairie Trails* is both a memorable portrayal of Canadian terrain and Grove's considered paradigm of the human experience.

We now know that Grove's imaginative gifts coloured his accounts of his own life, a fact that has given an added interest to this book and to his ostensible autobiography, *In Search of Myself* (1946). The same response has been extended to 'Grey Owl', the supposed Ojibwa publicist now identified as an Englishman, Archie Belaney, and more often dismissed as an impostor than discussed as a creative artist. Though he was obviously not in the same class as Grove, Grey Owl had his own personal vision of a somewhat idealized wilderness, and in *The Men of the Last Frontier* (1931), *Pilgrims of the Wild* (1935), and *Tales of the Empty Cabin* (1936) he presented it as a powerful imaginative myth. In so doing he caught the imagination of millions by means of an artistry that involved the remaking of self as well as a no-longer-fashionable travelogue rhetoric. He wrote the romantic elegy for a Canada that never was, but he also played an important role in what is now a respected struggle for the conservation of wildlife and natural resources. It was a role that demanded an Indian persona and he humoured the public by accepting the image they wished upon him. He was prepared to be a popularizer, even a romantic sentimentalist, if it served his ends, which were anything but ignoble.

In some respects, Grey Owl is part of a literary line from Roberts and Seton, as is clear from the following comment from *Pilgrims of the Wild*: 'The kinship between the human race and the rest of our natural fauna becomes very apparent to those of us who sojourn among the latter for any length of time' (Preface). Despite his denial of literary ambition or ability (part of his Indian mask), he was a self-conscious, florid writer preoccupied with rhythm and stylistic effect, evoking the romance of the wilderness with resonant phrases like 'the grim Spirit of the Silent North' or 'the magic lure of far horizons' (*The Men of the Last Frontier*, Ch. 1 and 2). This style can easily collapse into cliché, but at his best Grey Owl communicated an affecting if unsubtle charm.

Roderick Haig-Brown was another Englishman who felt the lure of the Canadian wilderness. In an early book, *Pool and Rapid* (1932), he similarly conjured up the 'romance' and 'mystery' of the wild (Ch. 17), but soon eschewed such rhetoric to write about fishing and British Columbia – and preferably both together – in a wonderfully lucid prose that seems effortless but is the fruit of a severe artistic apprenticeship. Growing up in Hardy's Dorset, he owed much to the great tradition of English rural prose, but he adapted it sensitively and aptly to his adopted country. He seems particularly conscious of a responsibility to justify his change of citizenship by a thorough mastery of the historical, zoological, and sociological aspects of the province in which he lived. He is one of the few modern Canadian writers whose favourite form is the non-fiction essay – and has been unjustly neglected by the literary establishment for this reason. Although he wrote animal stories and outdoors fiction for both adult and junior readers, his best work is to be found in his relaxed but authoritative articles on fish and fishing, especially *A River Never Sleeps* (1946), the four volumes devoted to the seasons of a fisherman's calendar, and the delightful collection of familiar essays collected in *Measure of the Year* (1950).

Like Grey Owl, Haig-Brown began as a trapper and ended as a conservationist, though he made the change more quietly and far less flamboyantly. Indeed, he was at his most successful when avoiding obvious effects. 'Neither sport nor art,' he tells us in *Fisherman's Spring* (1951), 'should be unnecessarily cluttered and complicated' (Ch. 6). He writes with care and judiciousness from his own experience, his prose as smooth-flowing as the streams he loved. He is a writer more often read for his content than for his literary dexterity, but the latter contributes much to the effective communication of the former. Finally, unlike many writers in this genre (and unlike many fishermen), he is scrupulous in differentiating fact from fiction.

All these views of the Canadian land have been provided by men who were, at least initially, outsiders. Another technical outsider, the American novelist and writer Wallace Stegner, has produced in *Wolf Willow* (1962) a classic text for the understanding of the Canadian prairies. Stegner grew up on the border between Montana and Saskatchewan, and his book, subtitled 'A History, a Story, and a Memory of the Last Plains Frontier', reproduces in a graceful and flexible prose not only the landscape of his own childhood in Whitemud (= Eastend, Saskatchewan) but the historical processes which moulded that landscape. Beginning and ending in the present (it is a geometrical book, following one of its main images), it probes back into the nineteenth- and early twentieth-century past to discover the forming history that was unknown to him when he was living there: 'We knew as little of our intense and recent past as if it had been a geological stratum hidden underground' (Part 2, Ch. 3). This is a characteristic experience – parallels are to be found in the responses of Kroetsch and Wiebe – and it applies more generally to the recent historical awakening of the country as a whole.

Wolf Willow is a central prairie document, at once a comprehensive image of the culture of the west (a much-needed alternative to Canadian history as seen from eastern Canada) and a creative brooding over the way in which past heroism and past shames develop into present fascinations and complexities. This is local history humanized and transformed into art; Stegner recognizes and provides an appropriate fiction to reveal the essence that history alone can never catch. *Wolf Willow* is unquestionably literature, not least because of what Stegner calls 'the fictional or poetic truth that I would rank a little above history' (Acknowledgments). His subtitle involves memory as well as history and story (an early reference to 'Proust's madeleine and tea', Part 1, Ch. 1, is neither pretentious nor accidental). Stegner has created a multifaceted impression of the prairie through its geography, its human past, its present look and smell (of wolf willow), and the creative unity we forge out of its separate aspects. As with Grove, this is a portrait of a land through the imaginative eyes of an individual and participating observer.

'The net of memory has a mesh all its own.' The phrase fits *Wolf Willow*, though it comes from Ernest Buckler's *Ox Bells and Fireflies* (1968, Ch. 15). This memoir is *The Mountain and the Valley* with the balance dipped towards non-fiction, though Buckler imaginatively shaped the book, as the opening sentences make clear: 'I'll call the village "Newstead", the boy "I". They stand for many.' His own description, 'novelistic non-fiction' (Cook ed., 137) is doubtless the best. It is a study in depth of Nova Scotian rural life. The subjects range from memories of school through varieties of work to politics, the rituals connected with illness, death, and religion, and the splendidly poised chapter on attitudes towards sex and love entitled 'Antics and After'. Buckler is at pains to reproduce the sharp vividness of recollection, the re-creation of a lost world in all its nerve-tingling immediacy. He is less cerebral than Stegner, and more self-consciously rhetorical (one of his most valuable sections is on the vitality of now-obsolescent rustic speech). As we might expect from *The Mountain and the Valley*, all this comes to us through a complex web of language. The book is packed full of unmistakable Buckler phrasing – 'I could see the map-red Micmac blood Rorschached on a folded leaf' (Ch. 2); 'people whose senses graze always in the same pasture' (Ch. 12); 'he took his sadness home like a parcel' (Ch. 18) – though he is often most effective with a pithy vignette or direct writing innocent of metaphor. Here memory is crystallized, transformed into a frequently magnificent, sometimes irritating rustic-rococo art.

But the master of this literature of the terrain is undoubtedly Farley Mowat, though his reputation as a successful journalist and controversialist has blinded many from recognizing the literary and creative aspects of his writing. Mowat's first love is the Canadian north, mainly because it represents the last wilderness available to his generation. He is fascinated by exploration of all kinds, and his work is unified by the image of the explorer. A considerable number of his books have been devoted to popularizing earlier explorers: his retelling of Hearne's story in *Coppermine Journey* (1958); *Westviking* (1965), his examination of the evidence for Norse voyages to pre-Columbus North America; and his 'Top of the World' trilogy, comprising *Ordeal by Ice* (1960), *The Polar Passion* (1967), and *Tundra* (1973), primarily anthologies of northern exploration accompanied by Mowat's own anecdotes and interpretations. In other books, essentially creative versions of autobiography, he is himself an explorer, whether physically or intellectually or both. He first achieved fame with *People of the Deer* (1952) and *The Desperate People* (1959), his presentations of the Ihalmiut Inuit of the Barren Lands which became exposés of white (Canadian) exploitation and neglect of native peoples. Though sometimes praised as factual reporting and sometimes condemned as uninformed fabrication, these books are in reality imaginative and creative portrayals of their subject. In both (though especially in the first, where he had fewer statistics at his command), he offers illustrative stories, appropriate parables. Whether events happened quite in the way Mowat reports them is less important than their function of communicating general cultural truths. His aim is not so much to persuade our minds as to arouse our imaginative sympathies.

Mowat's personal investigation of the Inuit situation created a moral indignation that ultimately turned him into a satirist. This streak shows up lightheartedly in *Never Cry Wolf* (1963), a book often misinterpreted as a probably perverse vindication of wolfish behaviour. In fact it is a subtly humorous analysis of human pride and foible in which Mowat casts himself in a role not unlike Gulliver's among the Houyhnhnms in the fourth book of *Gulliver's Travels*. He sets out to observe wolves and finds that he is being observed by them; he later learns to nap like a wolf and bases his fishing technique on their example. The book becomes serious when, with a characteristically Swiftian device, the trap is sprung. Mowat argues that as predators wolves cannot rival human beings: 'The wolf never kills for fun, which is probably one of the main differences distinguishing him from man' (Ch. 20). *Never Cry Wolf* is a fascinating cross between animal story, fable, and subversive satire. In *A Whale for the Killing* (1972), the satire has become decidedly darker. Mowat uses the incident of a whale trapped in a Newfoundland harbour and harried to death by the native inhabitants as a sombre parable: 'The riddle from the deeps was the measure of man's unquenchable ignorance of life' (Ch. 16). But it is also an attack on human interference of all kinds, including Mowat's. Calling in outside publicity and technology in a conservation attempt, he is appalled to see the media regarding the local people much as the local people regarded the whale. This is a justifiably angry book in which Mowat does not spare himself. It is a courageous expression of his conviction that 'life itself – not *human* life – is the ultimate miracle upon this earth' (Ch. 17).

Mowat brings together a remarkable number of strands that have characterized Canadian prose. For him, as for Grey Owl, the wilderness is endangered by the stupidities of civilized man, which have upset the natural balance. The flippant but amusing scenario of *Never Cry Wolf*, with its fun at the expense of a bumbling officialdom, is surprisingly close to Leacock. His general attitude to wildlife, especially in *A Whale for the Killing*, recalls Seton, Roberts, and the more recent work of Bodsworth. Most important, his constant interweaving of fact and fiction plus his habit of portraying himself as a half worthy, half ridiculous figure find connections as far back as Susanna Moodie. A slightly later book, *The Snow Walker* (1975), is a collection of short stories about the north, but, even when he is formally writing fiction, the didactic intent is similar. There is an impressive unity in Mowat's work, and this is achieved through a plain, unpretentious, varied prose that expresses a consistent and creative vision.

Much non-fiction prose in Canada, as elsewhere, is devoted to accounts of travel, both within the country and outside. There is naturally some overlap with the previous section, as in the case of Emily Carr, one of Canada's most distinguished artists who turned to writing in later life when ill-health made painting expeditions difficult or impossible. In earlier days (though not nearly as early as she claimed), she had visited remote settlements in the Queen Charlottes to paint Indian life and the decaying totems still surviving from a richer native past. Her first book, *Klee Wyck* (1941), the title reproducing her Indian nickname 'the laughing one', consists of an imaginatively transformed account of these visits. Here is a fine opportunity to compare her visual and verbal impressions, and in fact the sections that make up *Klee Wyck* prove to be literary equivalents of an artist's sketches. Carr writes with an unpretentious frankness and, like most painters, both simplifies and improves upon reality. Though her visits ranged in time from 1898 to 1930, the book suggests a continuous travel narrative, and these sketches are interspersed with others describing Indian friends she knew and liked elsewhere. But although superficially warm and positive – she told a friend that it was written 'for the pure joy of reliving and travelling among the places & people I love' (qtd. in Maria Tippett, *Emily Carr: A Biography,* 1979, 248) – *Klee Wyck* is implicitly as critical a condemnation of white indifference and neglect as anything in Mowat.

Her later writing, invariably autobiographical but spiced with patterned invention, contains highly readable prose remarkable for its firm brush strokes and a concentrated phrasing that reproduces a painter's keen vision. For the most part it is pleasant though minor work. But Carr displays her best qualities as a writer in the selection from her journals published posthumously as *Hundred and Thousands* (1966). This could reasonably be described as a book of spiritual travel. *Klee Wyck* had been artistically unified by recurrent images of forest and sea. Here Carr explains the mystical and religious awareness that these images conveyed to her. It is a painter's eloquently moving confession of faith that goes far towards explaining the vibrant quality underlying her art, especially those late paintings that communicate 'the glory of the woods' (12 November 1932). 'Real art', she insists, 'is religion, a search for the beauty of God deep in all things' (8 February 1935). *Hundreds and Thousands* is one of the most revealing accounts of visionary quest in Canadian literature. More justly than the *Klee Wyck* sketches it deserves her characteristically direct comment, 'I went down deep into myself and dug up' (24 June 1937).

As might be expected, some of the best non-fiction prose has been produced by novelists, and Hugh MacLennan's *Seven Rivers of Canada* (1961) is a notable case in point. Although his other work is overshadowed by the importance and appeal of his fiction, MacLennan was one of our finest essayists, and much of his non-fiction involves travel. Thus *Cross-Country* (1949) concerns itself with both Canada and the United States, while *Scotchman's Return* (1960) includes a characteristic essay about a return to the 'old country' of his ancestors. But *Seven Rivers of Canada* is his finest non-fiction achievement. At the suggestion of a *Maclean's* editor, he decided to investigate the main Canadian rivers and report on his findings. The resulting book is an exploration at once geographical, historical, and intellectual. One of the chapters is entitled 'The Rivers that made a Nation', and MacLennan is highly impressed by the implications of this phrase. He offers a tribute to the explorers who first mapped them, a celebration of the land they serve, and a plea to the nation to awaken to a sense of both its past and its present. 'Had this story been here all this time', he asks in the introduction, 'and I ignorant of it?' *Seven Rivers of Canada* is an informative yet intensely personal document. MacLennan writes of the people he meets, the sights he sees, and the history his readers had seemingly forgotten. He appropriately mentions Harold Innis (see p. 199) since the book is a literary by-product of Innis's work on communications. Written in a beautifully relaxed and limpid prose, this is one of the wisest books about Canada and the Canadian land.

A few years earlier, the expatriate Norman Levine had offered a very different travel report in *Canada Made Me* (1958). Levine had returned to Canada in 1956 to reconsider his native country, and toured from coast to coast on a decidedly limited budget. From a perspective influenced perhaps by shabby lodgings and restaurants, he produced a bleak portrait of Canadian philistinism: 'so much of Canada was just dull and boring' (Ch. 6). He seems to expect this and be resigned to it. As a piece of descriptive and atmospheric writing it is often highly impressive, conveying the same tone of melancholy loss that emanates from his short stories, though we are conscious here of a stronger tinge of cynicism. The bourgeois are dismissed as lifeless, the poor as degraded. But the sense of dingy monotony suits his temperament and his style a little too neatly; all his anecdotes conveniently confirm his preoccupations. *Canada Made Me* is a valuable document, partly because it presents an ordinary world that most travel writing ignores, partly because it was written just before the cultural awakening of the later decades of the century. What Levine observed is still present but it is no longer a deadening norm. In his social and local writings MacLennan roused his readers from the lethargy that Levine presented as seemingly inevitable and unchangeable. Together, the books succeed in taking the pulse of their age.

Of travellers abroad, writers well known in other genres have also produced the best non-fiction accounts. Margaret Laurence's *The Prophet's Camel Bell* (1963), an account of two years (1950–52) spent in British Somaliland where her husband had been appointed engineer in charge of water-conserving construction, is especially noteworthy. The book was written ten years after the experience, and we soon realize that it is far more than a record of travel in an exotic and rarely visited country.

From the start Laurence hints that it will reveal most about her own character. While we are assured that 'the last thing in the world that would occur to you is that the strangest glimpses you may have of any creature in the distant lands will be those you catch of yourself' (Ch. 1), we immediately become aware of a highly self-conscious writer clear-sightedly observing the effects of culture shock on her own attitudes.

For those interested in Laurence as novelist, phrases like 'burdened with baggage', 'bland as egg-plant', and 'stranger in a strange land' (Ch. 1) suggest insights and phrases familiar in her later fiction: at the same time careful readers gradually recognize a subtle progression within the book that reflects a characteristically Canadian tradition. Whether Laurence was conscious of it or not, her account shares many structural resemblances with Moodie's *Roughing It in the Bush*. The opening chapter is entitled 'Innocent Voyage' and she soon admits that 'every traveller sets foot on shore with some bias' (Ch. 2). She goes with simplistic Canadian-liberal notions of imperialism and colonialism: 'my feeling about imperialism was very clear – I was against it' (Ch. 2). But she cannot prevent herself from being addressed as 'Memsahib' and is forced, ironically, to behave in the way her servants expect. She is sceptical in religious matters, but in time comes to respect a faith which she can never share but which provides, in Somaliland, a necessary alternative to scientific materialism. And she eventually comes to the realization that 'we had all been imperialists, in a sense' (Ch. 14). *The Prophet's Camel Bell* is an honest and subtle book. The ostensible subject, bringing water to the Somali desert, has symbolic connotations which Laurence, characteristically, implies but never emphasizes. Instead, she paints a wonderfully deft self-portrait, with none of Moodie's clumsy and exaggerated effects, but the basic transformation from ignorance to chastened understanding is essentially the same. Only a mature and imaginative writer could have written it.

A decidedly more complex study in the relativity of cultures is to be found in *Days and Nights in Calcutta* (1977), written by Clark Blaise in collaboration with his East Indian wife and fellow novelist, Bharati Mukherjee. The book recalls what for Blaise was a fascinating but severely disorienting plunge into an utterly different way of life, and for Mukherjee an unsettling new perspective on her own culture after an adjustment to Western ways. Blaise writes the first part, Mukherjee the second; each claims to have written independently of the other, and the two versions, bound back to back, offer an intriguing and perhaps symbolic double focus. Occasionally the same incident or anecdote occurs in both, and revealing insights result from this unique form of intertextuality. Of particular interest to readers of Blaise's fiction is the smooth, almost imperceptible blend of one form into another. There is no reason to suspect that Blaise has transformed the autobiographical facts after the fashion of Grove or even Carr; rather, we recognize more clearly the extent to which he grafts his own troubled introspection on to his fictional creations. The book is able to probe deeper than Laurence's because Blaise and Mukherjee are *not* strangers in a strange land, though they are not assimilated either. They are within Indian life, but not of it; their perceptions naturally vary, but they both inhabit a kind of social no man's land between cultures. *Days and Nights in Calcutta* paints an unforgettable portrait of the crowded jostle and resigned fatalism of a hallowed yet, to the Western mind, inevitably alien civilization (its unknowable quality is what makes it so traumatic an experience for Blaise), but this is achieved through the keen-eyed honesty provided, in an apt paradox, by the two mainly fiction-writing protagonists.

While Blaise's generation was exploring the mysteries and challenges of the 'Third World', an earlier one was recalling the expatriate literary and artistic society of Paris in the 1920s. For Callaghan it was Ernest Hemingway's suicide that stimulated his re-creations of *temps perdu* in *That Summer in Paris* (1963). The subtitle, 'Memories of Tangled Friendships with Hemingway, Fitzgerald, and Some Others,' sufficiently indicates its main *raison d'être*, an attempt to understand the past by reliving it in the light of the present. But it gives Callaghan the opportunity to reassess his own career, to smooth the edges of his literary progress, and to assert a consistent development over almost forty years. Characteristically, it is convincing by virtue of its directness, its unelaborated no-nonsense clarity; at the same time, it presents a non-fiction counterpart to those fictive reconsiderations of the past so prominent in his later novels.

Callaghan's viewpoint is supplemented, however, by a much more ambitious piece of imaginative prose, John Glassco's *Memoirs of Montparnasse* (1970). Here we begin to experience a series of fascinating if sometimes accidental literary interconnections. Glassco, along with his friend Graeme Taylor, appears briefly in *That Summer in Paris* while both occupy centre stage in Callaghan's early short story 'Now That April's

Here'. In addition, they are portrayed in Stephen Scobie's poem *McAlmon's Chinese Opera*, which also re-creates these years. By the same token, Callaghan makes a brief appearance in Glassco's book. *Memoirs of Montparnasse* is unreliable as literary history, yet unparalleled as an imaginative reconstruction of its period. In his prefatory note Glassco describes it as 'my own *Confessions of a Young Man* à la George Moore', a clear invitation to read it as representative rather than literal truth. In form (though naturally in nothing else) the book resembles Grove's *Search for America;* both are semi-fictional versions of a phase of Western civilization in which the author/narrator offers himself as a significant example.

Part of the book was written between 1928 and 1933 (when Glassco was about to face a critical operation), but it is now known that, despite the author's claims, most of it was composed as late as the 1960s. Be that as it may, the book creates an illusion of youthful high spirits and engaging brashness that may be initially irritating but eventually proves disarming. On one occasion he comments: 'I was trying to write the third chapter of this book, and feeling handicapped by the recentness of events, I … was reduced to stating just what happened' (Ch. 13) That, however, rarely occurs. As a whole, *Memoirs of Montparnasse* both creates and fabricates the brittle splendours of an infuriating but fascinating long-vanished society.

The Canadian land is now mapped and explored, if not wholly tamed. But the intellect, as I have suggested, can claim its own beckoning frontiers – frontiers which are beyond the reach of rational control. Influenced, perhaps, by the traditional Canadian patterns of resolutely articulating into uncharted realms, other writers have been adventurous (often, indeed, controversial) in exploring mental terrains.

Such terrain needs to be approached cautiously, and before I conclude with a discussion of the more substantial intellectual monuments in recent Canadian letters, it may be as well to begin at the level of humour. Perhaps the one book that most obviously and brilliantly continues the Leacock tradition of humour and parody is Paul Hiebert's *Sarah Binks* (1947). In a country seemingly preoccupied with myth, 'the sweet songstress of Saskatchewan' has become an appropriately mythic figure. Hiebert's account of her life and work is a classic exposé not only of bad poetry but of bad criticism of all kinds – biographical, historical,

practical, etc. It ridicules pedantry, scholarly excesses, the special plead-
ings of enthusiastic nationalism, and above all misuse of language. The
reader is invited to adjust to a number of verbal romps, from Sarah praising the Northwest Territories where 'the hand of man hath never trod'
(Ch. 1) to the description of A. E. Windheaver as 'long since called to his
reward in the Canadian Senate' (Ch. 11). It is a good-natured but devas-
tating spoof on every variety of literary pretentiousness that all critics and
critical readers should take to heart.

Robertson Davies's non-fiction writings are also, of course, characterized by wit and humour. Indeed, some of his early books are the
product of his *alter ego* Samuel Marchbanks, who in diary, table talk, and
almanac, lashes the absurdities of his age with obstreperous verve. Since
the appearance of Davies's mature fiction, these books seem relatively
tame, but they served an important function in allowing him to rehearse
his satiric and tonal strategies. They make perfect bedside reading. In
addition, from a literary viewpoint they blend well enough into his later
discursive writings, books of literary and cultural criticism that display
wide learning and firm opinions in a polished and often sparkling style. *A
Voice from the Attic* (1960), in particular, is a deeply serious book about
books and literary taste that appeals to a genuinely humane and discriminating literary élite (in the traditional, not the 'postmodern' sense), but
Davies wears his wisdom lightly and proves that it is possible to be intelligent and cultivated without being either ponderous or dull.

Had Harold Innis been able to benefit from Davies's example, he
would have been far more widely known than he is today. Innis is
important in modern Canadian thought because of his central position
in a line of modern synthesizers. He began as a more or less conventional
economic historian with *A History of the Canadian Pacific Railway* (1923),
The Fur Trade in Canada (1930), and *The Cod Fisheries* (1940), but in his
later work, represented by *Empire and Communications* (1950) and *The
Bias of Communication* (1951), he broadened his horizons to develop an
expansive vision of technology and communications, the latter including
not only rivers, roads, and railways but the oral and written dissemina-
tion of information and ideas from stone tablets, papyrus, and
parchment to newspapers, radio, and television. Innis was well aware of
his paradoxical role as a wide-ranging synthesizer in a world of increasingly narrow speculation. These later books are for the most part

extraordinarily concentrated digests and combinations of others' find-ings. In some respects they are manifestations of the principle they illus-trate: modern technology has made information available to him in such quantity that he can only skim and select, always dependent on the accu-racy (or otherwise) of the authorities he cites. Yet Innis had the capacity to offer provocative hints that proved stimulating to thinkers and researchers in widely varied fields. He deserves a place here by virtue of his imaginative capacity to make connections and create intellectually exciting hypotheses. Unfortunately his style, which often consists of chal-lenging paradox heaped upon challenging paradox, is so close-packed as to become frequently enigmatic and sometimes impenetrable. As a consequence, many of his ideas fell on stony ground until popularized by the intellectual and stylistic pyrotechnics of Marshall McLuhan.

McLuhan's comparable development was from an original and inci-sive but not particularly unusual professor of English to a controversial theorist on print and electronic media who for many years was consid-ered the guru of a new world. *The Gutenberg Galaxy* (1962) is close in form to Innis's work, since it too is essentially a gathering of (not always very well integrated) information linked by audacious but sometimes mystifying McLuhanesque commentary. The chief difference is that McLuhan's extracts are as likely to be drawn from writers and philoso-phers as from historians and scientists. Nevertheless, despite occasional liveliness of style it is hard going for the average reader.

By contrast, *Understanding Media* (1964) is 'popular' in aim, and full of quotable slogans, like that famous combination of paradox and cliché, 'the medium is the message'. Whereas with Innis every sentence was a piece of discrete information, with McLuhan each was a witty epigram. Unhappily, the transformation, though it brought him thousands of readers, led to his downfall (the word is not, I think, too extreme). McLuhan's epigrams, like Oscar Wilde's, are outrageous and provocative but, again like Wilde's, often inconsistent with each other. It is easy to pick logical holes in *Understanding Media,* though McLuhan, who rarely deigned to respond to criticism, could shrug off such objections as the obsolescent prejudices of the linear mind. More important, it is fre-quently difficult to understand which side he is on. He often insisted (as have his followers) that he was appalled at the prospects of an electronic culture and was fervently exhorting his audience to understand it as a means of controlling its effects (e.g., 'Education is ideally civil defense against media fall-out', Ch. 20). But in Northrop Frye's words, 'McLuhan is caught up in the manic-depressive roller-coaster of the news media' (*Divisions* 37). It was not always the reader's fault if his 'probes' – provocative and often extreme hypotheses deliberately launched to test responses – were taken more seriously than they were meant. His witty sallies in colloquial idiom seemed to imply acceptance of contemporary trends, and he could rarely resist attacks on 'typically semi-literate book-oriented individuals' (Ch. 31). The intellectual who dabbles in anti-intellectualism is inevitably mistrusted. Moreover, he indulged in too many prophecies that have not been borne out by subsequent events. Small wonder that his popularity soon subsided, though the coming of the World Wide Web has led more recently to a revival of interest in his work. Whatever the ultimate verdict, however, he remains one of those baffling but significant figures around whom circulate the dominant ideas of their age.

Northrop Frye, as cartographer of the literary imagination, was a systematizer whose findings have earned him a secure place among the unquestionably important literary theorists. Although his influence is most felt in literary studies, his theories about the structure of the human imagination, the contribution of myth, archetype, and the romance form to an all-embracing verbal universe in which every work of imaginative literature can find its appropriate place, have widespread implications as his recent book on the Bible, *The Great Code* (1982), makes clear. His best-known books are still *Fearful Symmetry* (1947), about William Blake, and his comprehensive *Anatomy of Criticism* (1957). In the latter, as several commentators have noted, Canadian literature is conspicuous by its absence, yet it can be argued that Frye's 'Canadian-ness', observing the literary activity of the Western world from a periphery (from what he describes with typical dryness as 'a country which used to be at the edge of the world and is now a kind of global Switzerland' *(Divisions* 70), has made it possible for him to distinguish the universal wood from the local trees.

At the same time, however, in *The Bush Garden* (1971) and *Divisions on a Ground* (1982), Frye brought his synthesizing interests to bear on the literature of his native country, and some of his essays, notably the conclusion to the original *Literary History of Canada* (1965), are among the most influential in the field. It is, I suggest, because of the experience gained by considering world literature from a detached perspective that he was able to view his own culture (he tended to write 'culture' rather than 'literature' when discussing the Canadian situation) with a combination of native inner knowledge and the cool eye of one outside and perhaps above. He was primarily concerned with patterns and general trends. Like McLuhan, he was a slogan-maker ('where is here?', 'garrison mentality'), but his phrases, though often challengeable, are more useful and less distorting. His controlling myth belonged firmly to eastern Canada, and Canadians living west of Ontario are likely in the future to question some of his broader assertions. But he provided an important overview, a survey of the literary terrain upon which others can elaborate. Not least among his qualities are the piquant wit that enlivens and encapsulates his serious discussions and an enviable ability to express difficult ideas simply but (in the main) fairly. We read him primarily for the content, but the ease with which we continue to read is attributable to his style.

Finally, there can be no better way of concluding a chapter on Canadian discursive prose in a book concerned with the Canadian literary and cultural tradition than with a consideration of the agonized philosophical writings of George Grant, the grandson of George Monro Grant. With his deeply Protestant religious position and his passionately conservative political convictions, he was, of course, in no way typical of modern Canadian attitudes. But that is, in a sense, the point. A self-designated keeper of the Canadian conscience, as descendant of the Loyalist tradition out of which the idea of Canada developed, he was an embodiment of the world we have seemingly lost. A philosopher preoccupied with the break between religious past and secular present, he claimed that Canada was once 'a nation that believed that the past could tell us something of the future' (qtd. in Schmidt 25). If he is right, then his arguments are central to this study.

In an age of dynamic social action Grant was a believer in contemplation, in bringing traditional thought to the unprecedented problems confronting the modern world. He was a moral philosopher in the 'old-fashioned' sense of the term; in *Philosophy in the Mass Age* (1959) he icily dissociated himself from modern practitioners of the subject who 'spend their time proving that there is really no subject for them to profess' (Preface). But here we encounter the first of several paradoxes. Grant's thought embraces the traditional subjects of philosophy, but it grows out of immediate events. *Lament for a Nation* (1965) took its starting point from the political defeat of John Diefenbaker in 1963; *Technology and Empire* (1969) arose directly out of the Vietnam War. Both these historical origins represent aspects of 'a modernity which at its very heart is destructive of indigenous traditions' (*Technology and Empire*, 'Canadian Fate and Imperialism'). Against this human-oriented modernity (or 'liberalism') Grant insists on a religious awareness that sustained the past: 'we are not our own' (qtd. in Schmidt 63) but part of 'a moral order which man did not measure and define but by which we were measured and defined' (rev. ed. of *Philosophy in the Mass Age*, 1966, Introduction). Convinced of 'the barrenness of the all-pervading liberalism', he 'touched wonderful truths from our origins in Athens and Jerusalem' (*Technology and Empire*, 'Religion and the State').

Grant took his stand on principle. He was continually using those big words that make liberals (and 'postmodernists') so unhappy, or at least uneasy: the good, the sacred, the moral, order, restraint, justice, reverence, perfection. He even challenged the liberal (and 'neo-colonial') emphasis on rights, on unscrutinized freedoms. The danger words for Grant are modernity, technology, liberalism itself. Yet if all this sounds reactionary and backward-looking to undiscriminating believers in progress, Grant struck a perhaps unexpected, responsive chord in the hearts of the discontented young. His definition of God as 'the limit of our right to change the world' (*Philosophy in the Mass Age*, Ch. 6) made sense to a generation appalled by nuclear threats and the rape of the environment. A plea for the values of the past coincided with a realization that Canada possessed a past – a past that was endangered.

Grant was an anti-capitalist conservative, and because he was a direct descendant of the tradition that rejected the American Revolution he could become the intellectual representative of all those, whether on the political left or right, who were dissatisfied with the American-created 'liberal' civilization of the modern West. He used his historical Canadian perspective to view the social and moral world as independently as Frye viewed the world of the creative imagination. He was as concerned about the impact of technology as Innis and McLuhan, but he meditated upon it instead of amassing facts and theories about it. Like Grove, he respected 'the pioneering moment' (*Time as History*, 1969, Ch. 4) because it was seen as fulfilling the purpose of God, not catering to human greed, and he recalls Mowat in insisting upon our responsibility to the whole of life rather than just human life. We can thus see in his writings the intellectual and philosophical bases for a traditional stance that can be considered authentically Canadian. Above all, Grant made coherent sense of the interest in the past that can so easily become no more than nostalgic yearning; he exalted 'remembering' as a feeling back towards an awareness of perfection. If his vision sometimes appeared futile, even to Grant himself, it could show some heartening resilience. Thus *Lament for a Nation* stimulated a nationalistic movement at a time when it seemed to be writing the country's epitaph. His books belong to literature because of their eloquent and passionate commitment; to adapt Layton, he puts down his words in blood and would not be misunderstood. The very existence of a George Grant in the latter part of the twentieth century could be regarded as a substantial Canadian achievement.

A Note on the Contents of Volume Two

In the original edition of this book, the three main chapters on fiction constituted Part Three and preceded the chapters on drama and prose. For this two-volume version, it was found desirable to rearrange the sections, and as a result the chapters on fiction appear at the beginning of Volume Two.

These are followed by 'Twenty Years After', an update covering all genres and including a brief discussion of those whom I consider to be the most impressive writers to have appeared in the intervening years since 1985; a new 'Polemical Conclusion', which begins by reproducing the conclusion to the original work; and a brief appendix, titled 'A Note on "Postmodernism", Jargon, etc.' The volume concludes with a detailed Further Reading section, which lists works on individual genres, the main titles by individual authors, the most accurate and accessible editions of their work, and recommended biographical and literary-critical books. This section, at the time of printing, is the most up-to-date bibliography on the subject, and the most convenient guide for fuller exploration of Canadian literature.

Index

W. J. Keith was born and raised in England. He came to Canada in 1958 where he taught at McMaster (1961–66), then later at the University of Toronto (1966–95). Since 1995 he has held the position of Professor Emeritus of English at University College, University of Toronto.

His published work includes *Epic Fiction: The Art of Rudy Wiebe,* University of Alberta Press, 1981. *A Sense of Style: Studies in the Art of Fiction in English-speaking Canada,* ECW Press, 1989. *An Independent Stance: Essays on English-Canadian Criticism and Fiction,* PQL, 1991. *Literary Images of Ontario,* University of Toronto Press, 1992 and *Canadian Odyssey: A Reading of Hugh Hood's The New Age/Le nouveau siècle,* McGill-Queen's University Press, 2002. Mr Keith has also published poetry, most recently *In the Beginning and Other Poems,* St. Thomas Poetry Series, 1999.

W. J. Keith edited the *University of Toronto Quarterly* (1976–85), and was elected a Fellow of the Royal Society of Canada in 1979.